UMBRELLA
MIKE

UMBRELLA
MIKE

THE TRUE STORY OF THE
CHICAGO GANGSTER BEHIND
THE INDY 500

BROCK YATES

THUNDER'S MOUTH PRESS
NEW YORK

UMBRELLA MIKE:
The True Story of the Chicago Gangster Behind the Indy 500

car

Published by
Thunder's Mouth Press
An Imprint of Avalon Publishing Group, Inc.
245 West 17th Street, 11th floor
New York, NY 10011

AVALON
publishing-group-incorporated

Copyright © 2006 by Brock Yates

First printing, July 2006

Library of Congress Cataloging-in-Publication Data is available.

ISBN-10: 1-56025-776-8
ISBN-13: 978-1-56025-776-9

9 8 7 6 5 4 3 2 1

Book design by Pauline Neuwirth, Neuwirth & Associates, Inc.

Printed in the United States of America
Distributed by Publishers Group West

CONTENTS

FOREWORD

NO EVENT IN modern history rivals World War II in terms of altering Western civilization. Aside from the horrifying carnage around the globe, the social and political fabric of all civilized nations was changed completely with the rise of Communism and the ensuing conflict among nations known as the Cold War. But leading up to that cataclysmic period, the 1930s had a strange aura of their own. As Franklin D. Roosevelt's New Deal slowly lifted the nation from the long Depression and the rise of Nazism and Japanese Imperialism loomed on the horizon, Americans became fascinated with the talking motion picture, the glitter of Hollywood, and high society, while gangsters like Bonnie and Clyde, "Pretty Boy" Floyd, John Dillinger, and "Big Al" Capone competed for headlines.

The sports world was consumed with the power of the New York Yankees and the feats of Lou Gehrig and Joe DiMaggio at the plate, while in the Midwest the Indianapolis Motor Speedway was the site of the greatest, richest, most dangerous automobile race in the world. It was on that expanse of asphalt and brick lying in the Indianapolis, Indiana, suburb of Speedway that each Memorial Day men from around the world competed over the most challenging five hundred miles on earth.

Into this frantic milieu came a group of men led by a Chicago union leader named Michael J. Boyle, or "Umbrella Mike," as he was known. Boyle's power and prestige came from his ironhanded control of Chicago's International Brotherhood of Electrical Workers Local 134, but his passion lay in automobile racing and the urge to win the Indianapolis 500 Mile Sweepstakes. By joining with such unique individuals as the all-American boy Wilbur Shaw and the brilliant mechanic Harry C. "Cotton" Henning, Boyle then established a strange connection with a group of Italian craftsmen in faraway Bologna, Italy, to win the great race.

In conducting the research for this book, Fred Egloff, a noted historian of motor racing and western lore, sought to examine the files of the *Chicago Tribune* regarding Umbrella Mike Boyle. After gaining access to the newspaper's "morgue," he found that Boyle's file was missing, as were those of many noted gangsters from the Windy City's fabled era of crime. The disappearance of those files may mean nothing, but the coincidental connection to other shady figures in the city's past leaves multiple unanswered questions.

Crime, speed, and danger, plus a search for wealth and prestige, drove Boyle, Shaw, and their rivals to produce a scenario that was unique to motor sports and the nation as a whole. Welcome to the world of *Umbrella Mike: The True Story of the Chicago Gangster Behind the Indy 500.*

BROCK YATES
Wyoming, New York

ACKNOWLEDGMENTS

MY THANKS TO the following individuals, who made this effort possible:

L. Spencer Riggs
Donald Davidson
Joel Finn
Jeff Dworin
Patti Maki
Fred R. Egloff
Russell J. Ponder
Melissa Allen
Indianapolis Motor Speedway Archives
Ron McSweeney
Jim Fitzgerald
John Oakes

UMBRELLA MIKE

1

A GANGSTER'S HOBBY

MICHAEL JOSEPH BOYLE was a hard man among the beautiful people. He moved through the elite circles of New York society with little notice, as his sharply cocked fedora, his broad Irish face, and his ever-present cigar set him irrevocably aside from the celebrities and socialites who had left their Manhattan penthouses and North Shore, Long Island, estates to spend an afternoon at a unique automobile race being held on a newly developed road-racing course called Roosevelt Raceway. The July 1937 event, known as the Vanderbilt Cup, was to be a motor race unlike any other, bringing together the stars of the famed Indianapolis 500 and the International Grand Prix circuit in a three-hundred-mile shootout to establish world supremacy in the sport. Among the leaders of the contingent from the

Midwest was Michael J. Boyle—better known as "Umbrella Mike"—who had brought with him his driver, fellow Chicagoan Jimmy Snyder, and a brilliant mechanic from Missouri, Harry C. "Cotton" Henning, who would lay his magic hands on the "Boyle Special."

Mike Boyle had been entering cars in major races since 1926, when he was already established as the leader of Chicago's all-powerful Local 134 of the International Brotherhood of Electrical Workers. In the violent world of Prohibition-generated mobsters, Boyle had risen within the edgy embrace of the Capone mob and its rivals. Working hand in hand with local gunmen, racketeers, and bootleggers, he commanded virtually every aspect of the electrical business within the vast precincts of the Windy City. His nickname, "Umbrella Mike," had risen from his penchant for hanging an open umbrella on speakeasy bars to serve as a receptacle for cash payoffs and bribes from building contractors, judges, city officials, and others who needed to maintain peaceful relationships with his union. Operating in an urban cauldron of rival crime families that had seized power during Prohibition, Umbrella Mike established codependency and reasonable peace with the powerful forces of both Big Al Capone and archrival Roger Touhy.

These two mobsters, who dominated the Chicago crime scene in the twenties, were vivid contrasts in background and lifestyle. Capone wore his Neapolitan heritage on his swarthy face, accentuated by his puffy lips and heavy brows. A natty dresser, he never appeared in public wearing anything but flawlessly tailored suits and was surrounded by hard-edged men whose disheveled jackets concealed powerful handguns and even .45-caliber Thompson machine guns—known as "Tommy guns." A full-chested, powerful man, Capone was known to be physically violent on occasion, although he was seldom photographed by the adoring local press without displaying a broad smile.

Roger Touhy was the antithesis of Big Al, both in physical presence and lifestyle. Irish to the core, Touhy was scrawny and ever rumpled in off-the-rack suits. Avoiding the press, he worked behind the scenes in back-room speakeasies, issuing orders to his Irish mobsters, and was often on the move with a single bodyguard in an armor-plated Cadillac limousine.

There existed an unspoken peace between Capone and Touhy, having carved Chicago and adjoining Cook County into carefully controlled territories where the business of booze, gambling, and prostitution operated without interference, either from the two rival gangs or the heavily bribed and harmless police forces and local politicians. Umbrella Mike Boyle worked as an independent contractor in this edgy world, serving as a "bagman" to transfer solicitations and bribes between the two crime factions, artfully avoiding any disruptions of the uneasy peace that divided the great metropolitan area.

Like Capone and Touhy, Mike Boyle seemed to play his role more like a character in a Hollywood movie than as a real-life tough-guy union leader and crime baron. Round-faced, and with a florid Irish complexion, Boyle was a snappy dresser, always appearing in public in elegant suits with a vest encompassing his wide girth and gold-chain watch fob. An omnipresent cigar in hand, he moved in public with an expensive fedora or, on occasion, a classic Irish bowler jauntily cocked over his right eye. Unlike Touhy, Mike Boyle enjoyed the public attention and openly dealt with the local press as his power and prestige rose throughout Chicago, crossing the bullet-ridden boundaries separating the Italian and Irish sections of the city.

During the formative years of the American labor union movement, there was no avoiding contact with the powerful Italian and Irish gangs that controlled large segments of commerce in the major cities. Since the massive immigration surges of the late 1800s, the dark warrens of the poverty-stricken slums in New York, Boston, and Chicago had fallen under the control of well-organized mobs whose largesse created an ironclad loyalty among the simple, struggling citizens. As the union movement gained strength, these same blue-collar ethnic working classes became deeply entwined and loyal to the criminals who controlled vast areas of metropolitan America. From this unsettled, essentially illegal background, the great union leaders like Samuel Gompers and Walter Ruether rose up to claim legitimate and powerful influence over the domestic commercial and political scenes.

Umbrella Mike Boyle had been a union man almost from childhood. Born June 11, 1879, in Woodland Township, Wright County, in rural Minnesota, he was one of eleven children of Michael and Anne Boyle, immigrants from Ireland who were scratching out a living on a small potato farm. He was educated in parochial schools in St. Paul and at the age of sixteen entered the local International Brotherhood of Electrical Workers (IBEW) to learn the trade. By 1904 he had qualified as an electrician for the Chicago Tunnel Company, and on October 1, 1905, he joined the IBEW, ultimately becoming a business agent and vice president of the union that was to remain a major part of his life for more than half a century.

Among Boyle's pals and business associates were Spike O'Donnell, one of the prime instigators of the savage war to control Chicago's illegal beer distribution in 1926; James "Fur" Sammons, a psychotic killer who frightened even his employers in the Capone gang; and Roger Touhy, the murderous boss of the "Terrible Touhy" gang. Although aligned with the Irish mobs, which endlessly wrestled with Capone's Italian thugs, Umbrella Mike was able to move between the two organizations, keeping his overtly corrupt union outside their incessant gunfights and brawls.

Mike Boyle first made headlines in January 1907 when he threatened to call a strike at the National Electrical Exhibition scheduled for Chicago's coliseum. As union members of the Western Electric Company began to install new telephone exchanges leading to the giant building, he ordered them to walk out. With five thousand dollars worth of work to be completed before the exhibition opened two days later, the company attempted to hire nonunion electricians.

Convinced that they could buffalo Mike and his union, the Western Electric executives moved ahead with their nonunion workers plan until Boyle's men formed heavily armed picket lines around the coliseum. A few of the strikebreakers attempted to penetrate the union lines but were soundly thrashed with clubs and blackjacks. Understanding that the police would do nothing to stop the violence, and watching Boyle's forces increase by the hour, the management team held a conference in a nearby hotel. After a brief argument over whether or not to continue the head butting with Boyle and his gang, a truce was called. Mike was summoned to the meeting, where his demand for an instant wage increase was sullenly met, and the show opened as scheduled. This face-off against one of Chicago's most powerful corporations elevated Mike Boyle to local prominence, installing him as a tough leader ready to wage war on behalf of his union members, even against the commercial, industrial, and political elite of the Windy City.

Within ten years Umbrella Mike had become a major figure in Chicago's wooly world of gangsters, bootleggers, and corrupt politicians. The city was run by roguish mayor Big Bill Thompson, while the state was controlled by the equally thuggish Les Small, a former farmer from tiny Kankakee, Illinois. Both men were tightly linked with mobster Al Capone, against his enemy Diamond Joe Esposito, who was assassinated during the "Pineapple Primary" of November 1928, so named because hundreds of hand grenades, called "pineapples" because of their scaly, shrapnel-coated surface, exploded all over the city. This led a

Chicago Tribune newsman to compose a couplet that mused: "The rockets' red glare, the bombs bursting in air / Gave proof through the night that Chicago's still there."

By 1921, when Les Small first entered the governor's mansion, Boyle had teamed up with gangster Ben Newmark, the former chief investigator for the state's attorney, who had flipped to the other side, and the unbelievably viscous Walter Stevens, already dubbed the "dean of all Chicago's gunmen" and the chief hit man for the Capone gang. Starting as early as 1905, Stevens had charged fifty dollars for a kill and twenty-five dollars for "half a killing." Later working for Johnny Torrio and Big Al Capone, it is believed Stevens murdered somewhere around sixty men, although he served only one short prison term, which was suspended by Les Small. The well-educated Stevens was conversant with the works of Jack London, Robert Louis Stevenson, and Robert Burns. He neither drank nor smoked and forbade his three adopted children to read any violent or lurid books. As his daughters reached their teens, they were also forbidden to wear short skirts or makeup, even while their father continued his secret life as a gangland assassin and a friend of Umbrella Mike Boyle.

In 1931 Boyle's union associate Mortimer P. Enright, the chief electrician of the Chicago school board, was taken for a "ride" and found murdered in a Chicago suburb. It was believed that after Boyle had tabbed Enright as his successor, unknown rivals had killed him as a warning to the powerful union boss. Enright's murder, like most in the city at that time, remained unsolved.

Three years later, on August 19, 1934, a bomb exploded at the Edgewater Beach Hotel at Sheridan Road and Bryn Mawr Avenue. Two Local 134 union members picketing the hotel were slightly injured, and the assault, as expected, led to no arrests. Captain Daniel Gilbert, the chief investigator for the state's attorney, told the press that he had no intention of questioning Mike Boyle, although the union boss surely had an idea of who was behind the bombing. This was a classic case of Chicago's law enforcement of the day. Within the labyrinth of political influence that radiated outward from the mobs and unions to encompass the police, the city council, the state legislature, the press, and even some religious leaders, such incidents were quickly forgotten within the public sector.

While there is no evidence that Mike Boyle and his pals retaliated, there is little doubt that somehow, somewhere, a payback was made to whoever lit off the explosions at the Edgewater Beach Hotel. Such bomb blasts, shootouts, assassinations, and brutal beatings were so common in Chicago—and in other major cities—during the Depression-wracked 1930s that they hardly made headlines and seldom, if ever, led to arrests. It was in this lawless atmosphere that Boyle tightroped his way, somehow maintaining a peace pact with the warring factions that kept America's "Second City" on the very edge of the law.

As Mike Boyle rubbed elbows with the beautiful people of New York society who had gathered for the Vanderbilt Cup on that humid July afternoon in 1937, he had earlier that year wreaked havoc on his hometown after calling a wildcat strike. At eight o'clock on the evening of January 22, 1937, 450 of Chicago's 800 electrical workers had walked out after shutting off a series of circuit breakers controlling major segments of the city's power grid. In an instant, 94,558 streetlights went black, along with the traffic lights in the busy downtown Chicago Loop. Thirty-eight of the fifty-five drawbridges that spanned the Chicago River in Midtown were locked in the up position, jamming traffic for miles. Even the police force's internal telephone system went dead, leaving the police helpless to aid thousands of furious commuters who clogged the downtown streets.

"It's the city's funeral, not ours," smirked Boyle as frantic negotiations began with city officials, according to the *Chicago Tribune*. Within three hours his union's blackmail scheme had worked and power was switched back on. Such was the muscle of the International Brotherhood of Electrical Workers Local 134 and its boss, who now had five assistants to handle the millions of dollars in bribes that he controlled on what was an "official" salary of thirty-five dollars a week. When asked by an Indianapolis newsman how he could afford to enter powerful, rare, and fiendishly expensive race cars in the race known as the Indianapolis 500, Boyle had grandly swept his ubiquitous cigar and said, "It was with great thrift."

In 1917 Boyle had been indicted for a racketeering conspiracy involving restraint of trade—a constant issue in his reign as union leader. Part of the charge claimed that he had extorted twenty thousand dollars from the Chicago Telephone Company, clearing the way to construct a building without the threat of strikes. During a five-year court battle, in which Boyle refused to testify, U.S. Circuit Court of Appeals Judge Kennesaw "Mountain" Landis denounced him as "a blackmailer, highwayman, a betrayer of labor and a leech on commerce."

After being convicted in 1921, he was sentenced to a year in jail, but his power within the Democratic Party led all the way to the White House. After spending just four months behind bars, and relying on the influence of AFL (American Federation of Labor) union leader Samuel Gompers, Boyle received a pardon from President Woodrow Wilson and promptly resumed his union presidency. As a condition of his freedom, Boyle was required to pay a whopping five-thousand-dollar fine and was released full of rage over his imprisonment. Telling the the *Chicago Tribune*, "It's going to cost somebody something," he called a strike of Chicago's trolley cars for a day, a stoppage that critics claimed led to the death of a small child and injury to twenty people who were apparently using other forms of transport. The *Chicago Tribune* noted that he had lifted iron bars while in prison to gain physical strength and that his financial strength was now estimated to be worth more than $500,000.

Once free, it did not take long before Boyle was in the middle of another battle, this time involving gunfire. On April 29, 1924, police sought him in connection with a shootout that killed two men—Samuel Bills, the business agent for the Ice Cream Drivers Union, and IBEW member William DeVere. The mysterious shooting took place while

Boyle was holding a meeting just hours after calling a strike against the Illinois Merchants Bank building management. Bills's ice cream workers were planning a strike in an adjacent union hall. After the shooting, Mike Boyle "vacationed" in Canada for several months while his lawyers worked with openly corrupt governor Les Small and well-bribed city officials to keep their client free of any charges related to the incident, which remained unsolved.

This would hardly be the only time Mike Boyle was involved in shootouts. Not only did a number of his friends in the Chicago mob die violently, but in the winter of 1930, while returning home in his chauffeur-driven Cadillac, he was shot at four times by unknown—and apparently incompetent—assailants. He survived with only a minor wound in the stomach, while suspected members of the Capone mob—with whom Boyle was having a dispute—escaped without arrest. In the wild world of 1930s labor unions and organized crime, this was merely considered the price of doing business.

Despite the fact that Umbrella Mike was deeply involved with the criminal world of Chicago, he was strangely liberal in other aspects of his life, including his friendship with the black community. The first African Americans were welcomed into the IBEW union as early as 1919, an unprecedented act during a period of rigid segregation across the nation. The source of Boyle's liberalism toward black workers remains a mystery, except that he may have understood the latent restlessness among that segregated class and believed their talents might serve as a wedge to gain power for his union, as the barriers between blacks and whites were sure to collapse.

As the nation battled its way to victory in Europe in the waning months of World War I, Mike Boyle was also gaining enthusiasm for the new world of automobile racing. The Indianapolis Motor Speedway, nicknamed the "Brickyard," had canceled its Memorial Day five-hundred-mile racing in 1917–1918, but after the armistice on November 11, 1918, the management had announced that the great race would resume the following spring. Mike Boyle made plans to attend, having been hooked on the sport after seeing the famed Barney Oldfield break the one-hundred-mile-per-hour mark on the two-mile racetrack in the Chicago suburb of Maywood on June 15, 1915.

Boyle had traveled by trolley to the incredible track constructed from two-by-eight boards of Douglas fir laid edge to edge to form a smooth, high-banked speedway of a revolutionary type being built around the nation. Ironically, as his involvement with the sport increased in the 1920s, he never forgot his empathy for the black men who had tried to enter the lily-white world of big-time auto racing. Even the great boxing champion Jack Johnson had been banned from the sport, and other black drivers were forced to compete on rutted, cow-pasture dirt tracks in the poor, rural backwaters of the nation. During the 1920s and 1930s, Mike Boyle supported the Midwestern-based Colored Speedway Association and even sponsored a car in the series, helping several skilled but ignored young black drivers to win the championship. Both the

Indianapolis Motor Speedway management and the American Automobile Association Contest Board, which controlled major league professional racing in America, banned black drivers from competing. That color barrier was not broken until the 1970s, and during Boyle's time it was unthinkable for a young black man, no matter how talented, to enter the great 500. Surely if anybody had the influence to alter that policy, it was Mike Boyle, who by the mid-1930s had developed true political muscle throughout the Midwest.

It was during that period that the major Chicago newspapers began to refer to Boyle in such florid terms as "the Supreme Commander," "Dictator," and the "Strike Czar." When it came to any issue involving labor unions and the ongoing threat of strikes, sit-downs, or walkouts, there was no union leader to match the power of Umbrella Mike Boyle. For the next two decades he artfully managed to dodge prison, all the while working closely with "Little Tommy" Malloy, a brutal killer who had seized control of the city's movie projectionists union. Their plan was to jointly control the building trades unions in Illinois by relying upon Boyle's political connections with the overtly corrupt Governor Small (who, during his eight-year term, issued no fewer than eight thousand pardons to gangsters) and Little Tommy's strong-arm tactics. Boyle and Tommy Malloy would remain friends until February 4, 1935, when members of Frank Nitti's rival organization cornered Malloy's Cadillac on a Chicago side street and filled his body with machine-gun bullets.

Although most of his fellow mobsters and union hon-
chos spent their leisure hours and silly money at the
Sportsman's Park horse track, Umbrella Mike's first love
was high-powered automobiles—especially the exotic and
expensive racing machines designed and built by the
genius Harry A. Miller in his elaborate, surgically pristine
Los Angeles shops. As a sideline, and perhaps as a shadow
business for supporting his involvement in automobile
racing, he formed the Boyle Valve Company, a Chicago
firm that manufactured high-priced, well-engineered
engine valves for both passenger and racing cars. They
were well suited for competition and served as a sponsor
for Boyle's various racing machines. They would also be
widely used in the exotic Miller, Offenhauser, and Maserati
power plants entered at Indianapolis and other major
races in the coming years. Boyle also owned the Hen-
dricks Real Estate Company, which dealt in Chicago commercial properties during the 1930s, an apparently legal
operation.

Mike Boyle's love of high-speed automobiles had been
a lifelong affiliation. On Thanksgiving Day, November 28,
1895, sixteen-year-old Boyle had taken a trolley to the center of Chicago, where the local newspaper, the *Times-Herald*,
was sponsoring an auto race to be run on a 105-mile round-
trip between the Windy City and Evanston. This was to be
the first automobile race in America, and a dozen cantan-
kerous, flimsy machines entered the contest, which was won
by J. Frank Duryea in a machine of his own design and manufacturer at the stunning speed of 6.66 miles an hour.

The noisy cadre of primitive four-wheelers and their wheezing gasoline engines hooked Boyle forever. Before he was able to afford racing cars of his own in the late 1920s, he attended several races at the amazing Chicago Speedway at Maywood—a two-mile, high-banked board speedway where speeds of over one hundred miles an hour were recorded by racing stars of the day like Barney Oldfield, "Wild" Bob Burman, Ralph De Palma, and Eddie Rickenbacker. But because of the insane expense of maintaining the Douglas fir track, the Maywood Speedway lasted only three seasons, from 1915 to 1918. When America plunged into World War I, the giant track was torn down.*

At age thirty-six, Mike Boyle missed the draft and remained in Chicago, rising to power in the labor union world and retaining his enthusiasm for high-powered automobiles. As he gained prominence in the world of auto racing, he became a regular figure at such local tracks as the city's two indoor facilities—the Chicago Armory, at Fifty-second Street and Cottage Grove Avenue, and the International Amphitheater, where he first saw future star Jimmy Snyder. The young local driver would later join the Boyle Racing Headquarters Racing Team, as Mike so elegantly called his operation. Had not fate and the inherent dangers of automobile racing in the early years of the sport intervened, the legacy of Umbrella Mike Boyle in the history of motor sport would be radically different.

---

* The Maywood Speedway became the first site of the Hines Memorial Hospital, which is now the Loyola Medical Center at Ninth and Twelfth Avenues in the northwestern corner of the giant metropolitan complex.

In the dark year of 1937, the economic depression that gripped the nation had driven the brilliant Harry Miller into bankruptcy. Only a few men, like Boyle, were able to afford the luxury of entering automobiles in the Indy 500 and other races around the nation. Miller's shop foreman, Fred Offenhauser, was able to struggle on with the business, but limiting it only to building racing engines rather than the complete automobiles that were constructed by his boss. The broken economy forced even the richest car owners to keep running the same tired, battle-scarred automobiles for years on end, unlike the current atmosphere, where high-tech racing machines often become obsolete in a matter of months.

American professional motor racing in the bankrupt mid-1930s was limited to a few dirt track events on one-mile fairground ovals and the mega-rich Memorial Day five-hundred-miler at Indianapolis. The economy was shattered, leaving most of the population struggling to maintain a simple life and avoid the bread lines. But at the top lived a sliver of obscenely wealthy aristocrats, most of whom were still able to maintain a glamorous and elegant lifestyle even after the late-1920s stock market collapse depleted their family wealth. It was this tiny but affluent group that was to serve as the centerpiece for the strange events that had brought Umbrella Mike and his contingent to the decidedly foreign precincts of Long Island on that sunny summer day in 1937.

A group of prominent Wall Street businessmen had revived the Vanderbilt Cup race a year earlier in memory of the international competitions run from 1904 to 1916 by automotive enthusiast William Kissom "Willie K" Vanderbilt. They had spent $675,000 to develop a 270-acre plot of open land on the edge of Westbury, Long Island, adjacent to Roosevelt Field Airport that had served as the launching pad for Charles Lindbergh's famed transatlantic solo flight eight years earlier. The 1936 event, won by Italian racing champion Tazio Nuvolari, employed a serpentine, sixteen-turn road course that the New York press described as a "death circuit." In fact, it was so embroiled in twisty corners that even a master driver like Nuvolari, at the wheel of a powerful Alfa Romeo Grand Prix car, could average a speed of no more than 65.9 miles per hour over the three-hundred-mile distance. After the race, the press hooted that the "Madman from Modena" could have run faster on any of the area's newly constructed motor parkways than in the 1936 race. The organizers, led by former Vanderbilt Cup winner and successful entrepreneur George Robertson, modified the course for the 1937 event, set for Independence Day, slashing the circuit to a 3.3-mile layout with only seven sweeping corners.

But trouble lay ahead. Captain Eddie Rickenbacker, the owner of the Indianapolis Motor Speedway and a major celebrity, quit the board of directors after an internal squabble, as did George "Wetwash" Marshall, the commercial laundry tycoon who also served on the board. He was the owner of the National Football League's Boston Braves, who were soon to be transferred to Washington to become the Redskins. Even the sponsor of the event abandoned the show. George Vanderbilt chose to leave the country with his wife on an expedition to the Caribbean to hunt for seashells and other zoological prizes for the Philadelphia Academy of Sciences. This left his mother, the much-married socialite, Mrs. Margaret Vanderbilt Emerson, to represent the family and to present the winner's trophy. Worse yet, the expected presence of Nazi-sponsored German teams from Mercedes-Benz and Auto Union enraged metropolitan New York's large Jewish community and produced a widespread boycott.

The organizers had hoped that a surge of publicity before the race would increase attendance, but a stunning turnabout brought the event—and the nation—to a near standstill. Americans woke up on July 3 to read blaring headlines that aviation heroine Amelia Earhart and her copilot, Fred Noonan, had vanished in the South Pacific while attempting a flight around the world. This left millions of people glued to their radios for the latest news of the superstar, while rain spattered the Roosevelt Raceway, prompting a cancellation of the race. With New York laws forbidding motor racing on Sunday, the Vanderbilt Cup was postponed until Monday, July 5, when thousands of potential spectators would return to work.

Boyle and his little crew of Snyder, Henning, and two mechanics understood that they would play a minor role in the New York race, based on the publicity barrage being poured on the German teams and on defending champion Nuvolari. The year before, star driver "Wild Bill" Cummings had driven his Boyle-owned car through a white ribbon to formally open the Vanderbilt Cup revival. But this year he, Boyle, and the rest of the Americans were seemingly doomed to be defeated by the German superstars.

The two Mercedes-Benz and two Auto Unions carried outrageous swastikas on their silver flanks—like the giant German dirigibles that had been plying the Atlantic. Hitler's government had been supporting Grand Prix racing in Europe since 1934 with the intent to exhibit and promote German technology and to employ the racing cars as test beds for exotic alloys, rubber compounds, fuels and lubricants, and other innovations. For the first time, these teams had come to the United States, bringing with them their two best drivers—and archrivals—Rudi Caracciola of Mercedes (a Nazi hater who had moved to Switzerland) and Auto Union superstar Bernd Rosemeyer (an ardent Nazi and poster child for the so-called Aryan super race).

Facing this incredible array of talent and power, Boyle and Snyder were feeble competitors at best. Their now-aging Miller was unsuited for the twisty, 3.3-mile Roosevelt circuit, having been built for constant high-speed running at Indianapolis. The Miller's modest-sized brakes, three-speed gearbox, and large two-man cockpit (designed to carry a riding mechanic at Indianapolis) made the Boyle Special Miller a hopeless backmarker when facing the strong German contingent.

It was hardly the fault of Mike Boyle that his car was essentially useless against the foreigners. For years the two styles of motor racing on the Continent and in America had worked in opposing directions, creating massive differences in the way events were conducted and how the cars were designed. The contradictions could be traced to perhaps three centuries earlier when men raced thoroughbred horses. The Europeans raced their horses on grass courses, laid out on open fields and meadows long since cleared of forests. These meandering events, sometimes involving steeplechases and other obstacles, were perfectly suited to the vast estates spread over across France, England, and Germany. But as the colonials settled in North America, they faced millions upon millions of acres of forests, all of which had to be cleared for farmlands and settlements. There was simply no space available for the open, cross-country races of the types conducted in Europe, which led the colonists to construct dirt ovals ranging from a quarter mile to a mile in length. These racetracks were not only easy to create, but they were also perfect facilities around which grandstands were built and in which wagering customers were seated.

While in Europe horse racing attracted the "right crowd with no crowding," the Americans, who were more commercially oriented and seeking revenue wherever possible, went mad in the eighteenth and nineteenth centuries, building horse racing ovals in virtually every community, large and small. There being no such growth in Europe, it was logical that when motor racing became a sport around 1900, there was nowhere to compete, other than on public roads ranging from the perfectly manicured French *route nationales,* first constructed by Napolean, to the excellent Roman roads that coursed across Germany and Italy. Only in England, where until the early twentieth century ancient speed limits restricted automobiles' movement to a mere walking pace, did such open-road motor sports fail to flourish.

Meanwhile, in America the network of dirt horse tracks became the venue of choice for motor racing, meaning that the automobiles—running in counterclockwise circles at relatively constant speeds—were designed differently than their European counterparts. The American machines needed only modest brakes and relatively simple gearboxes, running as they did in a single direction and at high velocities. But the Europeans, needing to run on the open roads, had to build racing cars that were radical extensions of normal highway machines, requiring big brakes for downhill sections and hairpin corners plus multispeed gearboxes necessary for such circuits, often as long as twenty to thirty miles to the lap over hill and dale.

By the middle 1930s the cars that competed at the Indianapolis 500 were essentially country cousins to the sophisticated grand machines being run in Europe. Brilliant American designers and engineers like Harry Miller; the Duesenberg brothers, Fred and August; and Harry C. Stutz were every bit as smart and astute as their European rivals at Mercedes-Benz, Maserati, Alfa Romeo, and other car manufacturing companies. But they were creating cars to run at closed circuits like the Indianapolis Motor Speedway and on the high-banked board speedways that had burst into popularity in the 1920s. At these venues sustained speeds of 100 to 120 miles per hour were common, demanding engines and suspensions that could endure such sustained velocities.

At the same time, their European rivals were creating race cars that had similar speed capabilities, but such speed came only in short bursts as the cars had to negotiate slow corners over variable terrain. To compare the two types of machines was akin to comparing a marathon runner with a sprinter. Both were specialists, trained for specific venues. This was the case for the European and American racing cars that appeared for the Vanderbilt Cup, which, because of the international tendencies of the organizers, was more related to European road racing than to American oval competition.

It was into this strange arena that Mike Boyle and Wild Bill Cummings arrived on Long Island, their Miller highly outclassed by the smaller, lighter, more nimble Europeans with their huge brakes and multispeed gearboxes that gave them a huge advantage from the moment practice began. While European designers in Germany and Italy were creating machines with sophisticated independent suspensions using such advanced components as coil springs and torsion bars mounted in lightweight, tubular chassis, cars like Mike Boyle's rode on leaf springs that were little unchanged from those used on eighteenth-century buggies mounted on simple steel-rail frames. The German and Italian governments were supporting motor racing for propaganda purposes and therefore funded advanced research in such areas as supercharging, engine design, alloys, and fuels. But the Americans mired in the Great Depression had no such financial aid. Moreover, the American Automobile Association, which governed the domestic sport, had in 1933 rigidly mandated ultra-simple rules, banning such exotics as superchargers in the name of cost containment. There being no support for racing by either the cash-strapped Detroit auto industry or the Roosevelt New Deal, men like Boyle and Henning were left to fend for themselves, with no choice but to compete with essentially obsolete automobiles.

Nevertheless, the Vanderbilt Cup was a major motor racing event, and Umbrella Mike would not miss it under any circumstances. His star driver, Wild Bill Cummings, had won the Indy 500 for him in 1934, then ran third a year later and had been the fastest man at the famed Midwestern speedway in 1937 until a series of long pit stops for repairs dropped him to sixth in the final standings. But Cummings, a lean, handsome man sporting a pencil-thin mustache, knew that Boyle's hulking, outmoded machine was hopelessly outclassed at Roosevelt and had instead opted to drive for Californian Lou Moore, who had entered a smaller, lighter single-seater that had a better chance at competing with the high-powered teams from Europe.

Boyle replaced Cummings with a young charger from the Windy City named Jimmy Snyder. A diminutive, ever-smiling superstar in the exploding world of midget racing, Snyder was a devoted family man who seldom ventured out of the Illinois area and was known for his glistening leather shoes. It was said that Snyder couldn't resist passing one of the dozens of youngsters shining shoes along Chicago's Sixty-third Street. A member of the so-called Chicago Gang of midget racers, Snyder was on the verge of a meteoric career that would end with a fatal crash at a backwater track in Cahokia, Illinois, two years later. But at this point he was eager to challenge the best in the world, even at the wheel of Boyle's oversized, overweight ark.

The presence of the powerful machines from Mercedes-Benz, Auto Union, and Alfa Romeo did offer a tiny glimmer of hope to the Americans. The management at the Indianapolis Motor Speedway, led by Eddie Rickenbacker, had persuaded the American Automobile Association to alter the rules for 1938 to conform to the new International Grand Prix formula. The engine sizes would be 4.5 liters (270 cubic inches) unsupercharged, and 3 liters (183 cubic inches) supercharged. The Depression-based "Junk Formula" employed at Indy, which permitted large stock-block engines that were cheaper but less powerful, would be scrapped, and faster European cars would be eligible to compete at Indianapolis.

Mike Boyle, Bill Cummings, and Cotton Henning understood that obtaining one of the Grand Prix cars that appeared at Roosevelt Raceway would be the instant key to victory at Indianapolis. But how could they get one? In America a first-class racing car for Indianapolis was essentially available to anyone with a fat wallet. Engine builder Harry Miller made his racing power plants for anyone willing to spend upward of twenty-five thousand dollars, while a small group of car builders, based in California and on the East Coast, were ready to fabricate a racing car for roughly the same amount, giving rich sportsmen like Mike Boyle a shot at winning the greatest race in the world through other men's hard labor and talents.

In European Grand Prix racing the only serious participants were automobile manufacturers, who used the sport to promote sales and enhance their public image. This tactic was exaggerated to obscene proportions by the Nazi government, which subsidized Daimler-Benz and Auto Union for raw propaganda purposes, hoping to overwhelm potential enemies like France and Great Britain with the notion that the same German technology employed in motor sports was also in play with tanks, airplanes, and other military hardware. Automobile brands like Mercedes-Benz, Audi, Wanderer, and DKW were known to possess world-class engineering, thanks to the on-track triumphs of their racing machines.

So, too, for the Italian firm of Alfa Romeo, which was subsidized by Benito Mussolini's government, although at more modest levels than the country's so-called ally to the north. Other firms that engaged in International Grand Prix racing, such as the Italian Maserati and the French Bugatti, struggled against the power of the Germans in an atmosphere where independents like the wealthy sportsmen playing at Indianapolis were unable to compete on any level against the factories.

The German Grand Prix machines were never made available to privateers after they became obsolete. Every Mercedes-Benz and Auto Union race car was kept by the factories and either destroyed or placed in storage once they were taken off the racetrack. This was also true for the Alfa Romeos, although the Maserati brothers, struggling for income, did sell their older cars to private teams in

Europe and in South America. It was in this fashion that Mike Boyle was able to obtain his Maserati 8CTF ("C" for cylinder, "T" for *testa fista* or fixed head, and "F" for "formula"), two years after one had been first sold to Lucy O'Reilly Schell.

This schism in motor racing in the 1930s, where major European automakers competed in motor sports—both at the Grand Prix level and in sports car racing—remained until the 1960s when the formal ban on competition by the Detroit manufacturers was finally broken, first by Ford and then by General Motors and Chrysler. Until then the American Automobile Association had forbidden domestic car builders from competing, although the ban was consistently defied by sub-rosa support of independent teams, especially in the booming southern sport of stock car racing.

2

WEE WILBUR

THE ROOSEVELT AIRFIELD bordering the Vanderbilt racetrack rumbled with activity as the race teams gathered for the great event. On Friday afternoon, as rain clouds gathered over Manhattan, a single-engine, stagger-wing Beechcraft D-17 five-seater buzzed the track, its powerful radial engine rattling windows of the nearby Garden City Hotel, where most of the major teams and car owners had reserved suites for the weekend. Banking sharply, the sleek little biplane dropped lower and skimmed the long, 3,300-foot front straightaway, scattering a group of American Automobile Association (AAA) officials standing in the pits.

After making a second pass, the Beechcraft slowed, dropped its retractable landing gear, and made a smooth landing. Out stepped a small-framed, handsome man with dark hair and a pencil-thin mustache of the type favored by race drivers and movie stars of the day such as Clark Gable and Robert Taylor. The press was waiting. Wilbur Shaw was perhaps the most famous racing driver in America besides Wild Bill Cummings, having just won the 1937 Indianapolis 500 on Memorial Day in an automobile he had built himself and had brought to Vanderbilt the year before.

Shaw had nearly won the 1936 500 until loose hood rivets held him in the pits for sixteen minutes and sank him to seventh in the final standings. His attempt to run the car—sponsored by California oil baron Earl Gilmore—was a flop at the 1936 Vanderbilt Cup race, its front-drive system causing radical understeer on the second lap of the race and sending Shaw into the stout concrete barrier lining the track. Although he had done well at Indianapolis, Shaw understood his car's limitations at the Vanderbilt and in 1937 had left it home at his Indianapolis shop. His flight to New York was a long shot, a fling at obtaining a last-minute ride in the race based solely on his reputation as one of America's premier drivers.

As the diminutive five-foot, two-inch, supremely cocky Shaw cruised the garage area, joking with friends and examining the incredible Mercedes-Benz and Auto Unions that were tearing up the course with their awesome power, a stranger to the sport presented him with a bizarre opportunity. Enzo Fiermonte had arrived at Roosevelt with a fine race car, a fantastically wealthy wife, and virtually no experience as a driver. A handsome Argentinean

who had briefly contended for the light-heavyweight boxing championship of the world, he had settled in New York
and married Madeline Force Astor Dick, an older woman
with first-class credentials among the city's social elite.
Fiermonte wanted to race at the Vanderbilt, although he
had never driven faster than sixty miles an hour on public roads. His wife anted up the money to purchase a two-
year-old Maserati 8VRi Grand Prix car from friend and
fellow socialite George Rand, who in turn had bought it in
Italy after it had been campaigned with limited success by
the Italian Trossi-Torino Scuderia. With no place to practice with the unlicensed single-seater, Fiermonte first drove
it on the roof of the five-story J. S. Inskip car dealership in
Queens and then on back roads around his wife's estate
near Sands Point on Long Island.

Because of his wife's connections with the Wall Street
financial backers who had organized the race, Fiermonte
was allowed to enter the Maserati. Meanwhile, dozens of
other, more qualified gentlemen racers who ran with an
amateur group known as the Automobile Racing Club of
America were banned from the event for an alleged lack
of experience. On the opening day of practice on the
twisting, challenging Roosevelt circuit, Fiermonte wobbled crazily behind the wheel of the Maserati, narrowly
missing the fences and blocking the way for faster cars.
But thanks to the raw performance of the Maserati, Fiermonte still managed to qualify twenty-fourth out of thirty
entrants, although the cars he beat were hopeless dregs
from area dirt tracks that were present only to fill out the

starting field in an economically ravaged year when racing cars of all kinds were rare commodities. Fiermonte's qualifying speed was a full ten miles an hour slower than that of the pole winner, Mercedes-Benz superstar Rudi Caracciola.

A conference among the AAA officials and the race organizers determined that Fiermonte did not belong in the starting field, especially when a major talent and marquee attraction like Wilbur Shaw stood on the sidelines. The boxer was summarily replaced by the Indianapolis champion in what appeared to be a smart commercial decision. Little did they know it would have a major impact on the sport for years to come.

Wilbur Shaw was born cocky and retained incredible confidence in himself for his entire life. While learning basic mechanics in various machine shops and auto dealerships in Detroit and Indianapolis as a youngster, he had a single goal: to become a professional racing driver by the time he reached his teens. Hooking rides with clapped-out jalopies on dirt tracks around Indiana, Shaw quickly displayed skill, bravery, and bravado well beyond his years. That coupled with the innate mechanical skills he developed as a youthful apprentice labeled him as a superstar as the nation struggled out of the Great Depression.

Like many young men of his age, Shaw dreamed of escaping poverty through sports—in his case, motor racing. Thousands of others sought careers in baseball, the great and powerful national pastime played in every backyard and sandlot. Men like Babe Ruth and Lou Gehrig were among the most famous individuals, rivaling the top movie stars and politicians as their every move was chronicled in the daily press. Automobile racing hardly surpassed baseball in popularity, much less college football, professional tennis, golf, and horse racing, but for mechanically gifted, audacious men like Wilbur Shaw, the elementally dangerous and difficult sport was a magical door out of lower-class limbo.

After learning the trade in the Midwest, Shaw rode the rails to California, where motor racing boomed at such wide-open tracks as the Legion Ascot five-eighth-mile dirt track in the Los Angeles suburb of Alhambra. Built in 1924 by the local American Legion post, the Ascot became the epicenter of motor racing in Southern California and one of the most lethal tracks in history. Somehow Shaw managed to survive numerous crashes there, two of which killed superstars Bob Carey in 1933 and Al Gordon three years later. The constant crashes finally brought the *Los Angeles Times* into play, where an editorial bombardment ultimately forced closure of the Legion Ascot Speedway, its demise capped by an arsonist burning down the grandstands in the winter of 1936–1937. As public pressure increased and crowds dwindled, the Legion post finally closed the track in 1940 and converted the acreage to suburban housing tracts.

It was during this period that the deaths being recorded on racetracks around the nation brought numerous attempts in state legislatures, and even in

Congress, to ban racing of all types. It is possible such laws would have been enacted had the nation not been plunged into war in December 1941. It was then that men like Shaw, based on their reputations as expert mechanics, were absorbed into the war effort and their dangerous pasts quickly forgotten.

A native of tiny Shelbyville, Indiana, Warren Wilbur Shaw was born on October 13, 1902, and rose out of a broken family whose father had left them destitute. Dropping out of school and riding the rails back and forth between factories in Detroit and Indianapolis, he developed his inborn aptitude for technical workings and by his late teens was competing with a home-built car on the dirt tracks of the Midwest. An obvious talent, Shaw quickly rose to prominence, and by the early 1930s he was at the top level of the sport. He had miraculously survived a terrifying spill in 1932 at the Indianapolis Motor Speedway when his car soared thirty feet over the retaining wall. The crash broke neither his bones nor his spirit, and he went on to win the great race five years later.

Shaw had also experienced a bizarre crash on the sands of Daytona Beach, Florida, where in the 1920s numerous assaults on land speed records were tried. In the winter of 1927 Shaw had taken his Miller-powered Whippet Special that he had campaigned on Midwestern dirt tracks to the famous beach, planning to set a speed record for four-cylinder cars. Running well over one hundred miles an hour, the car caught fire. In order to douse the flames and escape injury, Shaw drove his car into the Atlantic surf.

Despite anything that could remotely be described as a formal education, Shaw's natural intelligence elevated him beyond his hardscrabble origins. Handsome, with a square-jawed resemblance to movie star Clark Gable, and amazingly articulate, Shaw was able to move easily among the wealthy men who owned the first-class racing cars of the day.

Although automobile racing of the 1920s and 1930s was viewed as a blue-collar sport, with the star drivers generally coming from lower-class backgrounds, the men who owned the machines were generally wealthy playboys who chose motor sport rather than the conventional gentlemen's hobby of horse racing. The purchase of a Miller, Duesenberg, or European Mercedes-Benz, Maserati, or Bugatti cost between fifteen thousand dollars and fifty thousand dollars (upward of five hundred thousand dollars in today's inflated currency), making them unavailable to all but the richest of sportsmen. In addition to the purchase of the car, a crew of expert mechanics had to be hired. Any winnings were shared, with the driver generally getting 40 percent and the owner 60 percent, from which he paid the crew and for the maintenance of the car. In the end, it was a minimally profitable venture, engaged in for sheer sport as opposed to any remotely sensible investment opportunity. However, if a driver of Shaw's talent could garner a "ride" in a first-class machine and avoid crashes, a reasonable living could be made from the vagabond life that involved constant travel and the everyday presence of injury or death.

Despite the strange crash at Daytona Beach and the wild 1932 tumble at Indianapolis, plus numerous other spills in his early career, Shaw managed to complete a twenty-year career in the world's most dangerous sport without injury until his final drive on Memorial Day of 1941.

Wilbur Shaw was thirty-five years old when he arrived at Roosevelt Raceway. He was a well-liked and respected member of the small cadre of American professionals whose sole source of income was the evil, elementally dangerous sport/business of professional racing. As an example, no fewer than eighteen men had died at the Indianapolis Motor Speedway since 1930. Seat belts were seldom used, the wisdom of the day maintaining that being ejected from an accident was safer than staying with the car.

After his crash at Indianapolis in 1932, Shaw had pioneered the use of a motorcycle crash helmet. His rivals derided him as a sissy and continued to race only with linen aviator's caps to keep their hair in place. Twenty more years would pass before crash helmets were employed in Europe, while Shaw's example led most American drivers to adapt the so-called brain buckets before the end of the 1930s. Fire was a constant threat, with the cars carrying as much as seventy gallons of gasoline or methanol in unprotected tanks behind the drivers, all of whom competed in shirtsleeves or loose cotton overalls. Little wonder that the fatality rate for race drivers was higher than any other sport or occupation in the civilized world. It was during this period that the great novelist

Ernest Hemingway observed, "There are only three sports: mountain climbing, bullfighting, and auto racing; all the rest are merely children's games."

Like Cummings, Shaw understood that the power, speed, and agility of the German Grand Prix machines were light-years ahead of American machines in terms of technology. The lightweight alloy chassis, independent suspensions, giant brakes, and multispeed gearboxes of the German cars elevated them to new heights of performance. To be sure, the Miller-based engines of the American cars were essentially equal, but the European chassis technology simply outclassed anything being developed in the United States.

Several American drivers, including California star Rex Mays and the wild-driving Billy Winn (who was believed to be hooked on amphetamines), were able to stay with the Germans in practice, based on their brilliant broad-sliding through the corners. Mays also benefited from driving a year-old Alfa Romeo Grand Prix machine purchased by West Coast promoter "Hollywood" Bill White from the factory after its participation in the 1936 race. A master driver, Mays qualified his Alfa third in the field and, after dogging the Germans for the entire race, would finish in that position. Winn, at the wheel of his own Miller sprint car minus a gearbox and proper brakes, ran among the leaders for eight wild laps, amazing the Europeans by driving sideways through the corners until he retired with a broken engine.

Wilbur Shaw quickly adapted to the Fiermonte Maserati,

using its four-speed gearbox with alacrity to power the machine through the field. But within a few laps the right-side exhaust pipe shook loose, forcing him to inhale invisible clouds of carbon monoxide. Unable to repair the damage, he soldiered on for the entire ninety-lap race, fighting a savage headache and blurred vision. He still managed to finish ninth, well behind the winner, Bernd Rosemeyer's victorious Auto Union, but on the heels of his friend Bill Cummings in eighth place and Joel Thorne, who had driven to seventh in an aged Alfa Romeo P3 Grand Prix car.

Shaw's tiny frame had surely contributed to his near-asphyxiation. Being seated deep in the Maserati's cockpit, he was positioned out of the airstream that might have swept away the fumes. It had not been the first time that his size had caused similar suffering. Shaw's first involvement with Umbrella Mike had come on Labor Day weekend in 1929 at the high-banked one-and-a-quarter-mile board speedway in Altoona, Pennsylvania. With Boyle's star driver, Cliff Woodbury, still recovering from an earlier crash at the same track that had killed defending Indianapolis 500 Champion Ray Keech, the diminutive Hoosier was given his first shot at the big time. But the America Automobile Association officials who ran the event claimed that Shaw, who had raced so-called outlaw tracks without AAA sanction, was too "inexperienced" to run with the established stars. When Boyle argued that Shaw was a rising talent, the officials relented, letting him start at the back of the pack. Furious at the slight, Shaw, driving Boyle's front-drive Miller like a maniac, charged through the field to lead by two laps. But a tiny screw had unwound on the Miller engine's supercharger, spitting a fog of fuel into Shaw's face. Groggy and sick, he rolled into the pits and gave up the cockpit to Deacon Litz, a large man whose head was in the airstream and above the noxious emission snorted by the tiny Shaw. Shaw was taken to a local hospital, where he was treated with a weird elixir of ammonia, water, and straight gin!

On March 15, 1930, Cliff Woodbury, who had decided to retire after his Altoona accident, persuaded Boyle to take the Miller to Daytona Beach in search of international speed records on the hard sand. Perhaps responding to the threat imposed by the impetuous Shaw on his reputation as Boyle's best driver, Woodbury powered the small, ninety-one-cubic-inch machine prepared by Cotton Henning down the beach at the astounding speed of 180.9 miles per hour. But regardless of his Altoona performance, Shaw's involvement with Boyle was short-lived and would not resume for nearly another decade. Knowing that he lacked the size and strength of many of his rivals, Shaw became a physical fitness advocate, running and building a stationary steering wheel mounted to a shock absorber that he spun endlessly to develop upper body strength.

Flying home to Indiana from the Vanderbilt, Shaw began devising plans to obtain a European Grand Prix machine for the Indianapolis 500. So did Mike Boyle, who had watched his driver, Jimmy Snyder, struggle with his oversized machine for thirty-nine laps until its inadequate three-speed transmission gave up under the constant shifting. Understanding that the German operations—Mercedes-Benz and Auto Union—would never sell their race cars to independent customers, Boyle, Shaw, Cummings, and the rest of the Americans knew that only two Italian sources existed: the Milan-based passenger car manufacturer, Alfa Romeo, and the tiny family-operated Maserati firm in Bologna. The drivers believed they could only dream of obtaining such machinery, but Mike Boyle was devising a realistic plan, based on his deep pockets and, perhaps, some special Italian connections.

Here the story becomes blurred. In Shaw's 1955 autobiography, he claims that a conversation with Mike Boyle before the 1937 Vanderbilt Cup race led to the purchase of the Maserati Grand Prix car that would ultimately bring him fame and two victories at Indianapolis. But in many ways this assertion makes no sense, because Bill Cummings was Boyle's premier driver at that time. To be sure, he had abandoned Boyle's big Miller to young Jimmy Snyder for the Vanderbilt race, but Cummings was contracted to drive for Umbrella Mike in the 1938 Indy 500, and there is no reason to believe that Shaw, a close friend of Cummings, would have intervened in Boyle's plans to purchase a European automobile. In fact, most historians are convinced it was Bill Cummings, not Wilbur Shaw, who would have been assigned to any Maserati that Mike Boyle was able to obtain. However, a series of strange and unfortunate events would alter the scenario and ultimately link Shaw and the Boyle Maserati in an immortal bond.

3

THE ITALIAN CONNECTION

HARRY CHARLES "COTTON" Henning was born in the tiny village of Alma, Missouri, in 1896, when the automobile was in its infancy. By the time he reached his teenage years, Henning was immersed in the world of cars, both as a brilliant, instinctive mechanic and as a fledgling race driver on backwater Midwestern dirt tracks. His first exposure to the big time was in the role of a riding mechanic, a dangerous and superfluous job that remained a part of motor sports until the late 1930s, when it was finally decided that the useless exposure of a hapless passenger to death and injury had to be banned forever.

A large man with an expanding paunch and thinning gray hair, Henning decided that his size and weight, coupled with the lunatic danger of riding with no purpose in a speeding automobile on the ragged edge of control, forced him to seek other employment. Latently talented as a mechanic, Henning was quickly hired by various racing teams to service and maintain their exotic machinery, which demanded constant attention.

Having given up sharing the cockpit by the early 1920s, Henning quickly took on the role of chief mechanic at Indianapolis and on the hyper-speed, high-banked board speedways that dotted the nation until their rotting wood surfaces and the Depression spelled their doom. His first major victory came in 1925 at the Indianapolis 500 when he handled the maintenance chores for Peter de Paolo's Duesenberg. In 1934 Henning established a strong relationship with Mike Boyle, maintaining his multicar team in an elaborate shop near the Methodist Hospital off Sixteenth Street adjacent to the Indianapolis professional baseball team's park. It was there that Henning prepared the front-drive Boyle Valve Special for winner Wild Bill Cummings that same year.

Henning was a stickler for detail and prided himself on his pristine workshop, where he told visitors, "There is a place for everything and everything is in its place." Because of its location near the great motor speedway, Henning's shop was a gathering point for members of the racing fraternity throughout the years, prompting it to be nicknamed "Henning's Hash House" by insiders, although food was never allowed inside the sanitary environs.

While Cotton Henning was listed as the "official" entrant, the Valve Special belonged to Mike Boyle, who, during his years at the speedway, entered cars under both his and Henning's names, apparently based on his unpredictable relationship with the law and the Chicago underworld. It is believed that one particular gentleman who witnessed Bill Cummings' Indy win in 1934 was an even more famous local native. He had entered the speedway race day crowd of more than 140,000 people—the largest attendance ever at any American racing event up to then—apparently in disguise. No one in the giant throng recognized him, or if they did, his presence was never revealed to the police. At the time, the man was FBI boss J. Edgar Hoover's "Public Enemy Number One" (or to many Midwesterners, a "modern-day Robin Hood"). John Herbert Dillinger, the notorious bank robber, had only a few months to live before being killed in a gun battle with G-men outside a Chicago movie theater.

Wild Bill Cummings came by his nickname honestly. In 1935 he had opened a bar on the Indianapolis west side called the Lucky 7—his favorite number and the one carried on his winning Miller race car. One evening Cummings rode his Harley-Davidson motorcycle through the saloon's front door and, in a series of noisy, high-powered spins, skated around the barroom, scattering tables and sending customers rushing for the exits. When he finally slowed to a stop at the bar and ordered a double gin and tonic, a friend asked him why he had nearly wrecked his own establishment. Laughing hard and taking a long drink, Cummings said, "Hell, because I can afford it now," he told the *Indianapolis Star* in 1935.

Drinking and driving in the 1930s was hardly considered the overt evil of today, and Bill Cummings hit the bottle hard, both before and after his appearance at the 1937 Vanderbilt Cup. He and Henning returned to the Boyle team for the 1938 Indianapolis 500, but his luck turned sour when the car's radiator sprung a leak on the seventy-second lap. He had chosen to drive his old Boyle Miller—now converted to a single-seater based on the new international racing rules employed at Indianapolis—after rejecting Boyle's first attempt to secure a Maserati Grand Prix car.

Automotive technology was essentially in stasis, based on the worldwide economic slump and the growing concentration by the engineering communities in all Western nations—and Japan—to develop advanced aircraft and tanks for what most military experts believed to be an inevitable resumption of the world war that had dribbled to an unresolved conclusion in 1918–1919. Racing cars, save for the radical advances being devised by the German teams, were essentially unchanged since the 1920s.

While the Nazi-backed Mercedes-Benz and Auto Union race cars employed such advanced components as fuel-injected engines, independent coil spring suspensions, multispeed gearboxes, and light alloy space frames, the money-starved American operations, such as they were, competed with automobiles that were in many ways dated, in terms of technology, to the early days of the automobiles and even to horse-drawn carriages. They still used leaf springs, while the axles were solid front and rear, with little suspension movement. The frames were constructed of twin steel rails, carrying aluminum hand-formed bodies that had often been converted from two-seaters to a single-seater and repeatedly rebuilt and repaired after wrecks, which were a common component of the competition.

Only the American engines built by the likes of Harry Miller, the Duesenberg brothers, and Fred Offenhauser were of contemporary design and equal to the best in Europe. However, Indianapolis 500 rule makers, reacting to the sagging economy of the Depression, had imposed a regulation that low-octane pump gasoline be used, while supercharging was banned for much of the 1930s. It was not until 1938 that the American Automobile Association and speedway management rejected such archaic restrictions and accepted the international regulations permitting exotic fuels and supercharged engines of a displacement up to three liters (183 cubic inches).

Unlike the racing cars of today, with their carbon-fiber chassis and lightweight running gear, which are designed to last for only a few events before being scrapped, Boyle's automobiles often remained in action for decades. Cummings's winning car of 1934 had in fact been built by Harry Miller in 1928. Boyle's star driver of that earlier day was Cliff Woodbury, who won the pole position at Indianapolis in 1929 (but crashed on the third lap) and had won several major board track races in the car. The Miller was then converted, and repowered with a larger engine, to a two-man machine according to the much maligned Indianapolis "Junk Formula." In that configuration it carried Cummings to victory before being rebodied for a third time in 1938, when the rules again required single-seat machines. Amazingly, the car ran in the Indy 500 and elsewhere until 1947, when it was entered in the 500 under Cotton Henning's name and driven to fifth place by young star Jimmy Jackson, who had finished second in the same car the year before. By then the aged machine was on the verge of celebrating its twentieth birthday and retired from competition. It remains, with its vivid green design, in the private collection of William Miller in Frankfort, Indiana.

Boyle refused to cease his search for a European replacement for his successful but aging Cummings Miller, even after Henning was flatly turned down by the Alfa Romeo works when he sought by cable to purchase one of the Tipo 308 eight-cylinder Grand Prix cars being planned for the 1938 season. This was a blessing in disguise in that the Tipo 308 was such a disaster that no one at Alfa Romeo or in its politically ravaged racing operation would even admit to the design. The chassis flexed so violently that even superstar Tazio Nuvolari could not control it. He broke his long and successful relationship with the company, pledging never to drive an Alfa Romeo again, and remained true to his word until his death in August 1953, after suffering a stroke nine months earlier.

Henning's next cable was sent to the Maserati brothers and their struggling firm in Bologna. They were in the midst of designing a three-liter, supercharged straight-eight-powered car for the upcoming 1938 season and via return cable indicated that one of the four cars being planned (although only three would ever be built) might be for sale. However, the brothers warned that perhaps a year would pass before a car would be available, and they suggested that a 1.5-liter supercharged 6CM Voiturette ("small car") single-seater might be a reasonable replacement.

While some historians believe that the Maserati brothers snookered Henning by selling him the small, 175-horsepower car, others think that, based on the intense pressure from Boyle to obtain a European machine at all costs, Henning gambled that the 6CM, thanks to its light weight, excellent fuel mileage, and superb handling, could be competitive with the larger cars at the motor speedway. The true story, according to Maserati expert Joel Finn, whose research on the subject is extensive (and who owns one of the three 8CTFs), involves the brothers offering the 6CM to Henning with the proviso that if another 8CTF were to be built, or one of the three designated for Italian customers were to become available, the 6CM would be traded for the larger, more powerful machine. Agreeing to the arrangement, Cotton Henning purchased the smaller 6CM for the 500. This agreement would be honored two years later. The 6CM arrived at the Henning shop in early 1938 to find Bill Cummings furious at the prospect of driving such a tiny, underpowered automobile. He chose instead to drive his old, dependable, rebodied Miller.

But despite its diminutive size, the Maserati 6CM performed well. Detroiter Mauri Rose (who in those politically incorrect days was often referred to in the press as a "Jewish" race driver) was selected as its driver. Rose had driven one of the aged Maseratis like the Shaw/Fiermonte at the Vanderbilt race and happily took on the challenge of driving the 6CM. He qualified ninth out of thirty-three cars for the 1938 Indy 500 and ran in the top ten until the overstrained little machine coughed up its supercharger at 165 laps.

Now convinced more than ever of the potential of a full-sized Maserati Grand Prix car, the Boyle-Cummings-Henning triumvirate made plans to purchase a proper model. In the Depression year of 1938 the worldwide car business was in terrible shape. Dozens of manufacturers had either closed their doors or were on the verge of bankruptcy. There were only a handful of European automobiles in the United States. Beyond a few Rolls-Royce limousines belonging to New York socialites and Hollywood elites, some British sports cars—MGs, Rileys, Lagondas, and others—a tiny collection of rare French Bugattis, and an equally sparse number of Italian Alfa Romeos, all owned by wealthy sportsmen in exclusive suburbs of the nation's largest cities, imported automobiles owned were virtually unknown in America.

There being no dealerships, much less a factory representative for Maserati in the United States, Henning had two choices for obtaining one of the automobiles: either negotiate again by cable, or board a ship and go directly to the Maserati factory in northern Italy. The first option having already produced the undersized 6CM, Henning was left with no choice but to make the arduous journey to Italy, where, if possible, a real contender to win the Indianapolis 500 might be purchased. After more meetings with Boyle, Henning received the lavish sum of three thousand dollars to pay for his trip and accommodations, plus a bank note for five thousand dollars that could be used as a down payment on a Maserati, presuming Henning was convinced such a machine could be a contender at Indianapolis.

By this time Boyle was obsessed with a desire to dominate the Indianapolis 500. Knowing that his current stable of racing cars was essentially obsolete, he would either have to employ one of a small group of American fabricators to create new and more advanced automobiles or seek an exotic alternative like the Maserati. The urgency of his mission only increased as word arrived that several of his rivals based in California, where dozens of brilliant designers, engineers, and fabricators operated, were planning major assaults on Indianapolis with advanced machinery employing the latest engine and suspension systems. Having no such manufacturing capability, Mike Boyle had no choice but to purchase automobiles built by someone else—in this case a group of brothers in faraway Italy. Meanwhile, men who were equally rich and powerful were preparing to leave Umbrella Mike Boyle and his celebrated but obsolete "Racing Headquarters" in the dust.

4

A WILD MAN ARRIVES

EVEN IF A majority of Depression-ravaged American racing operations were too poor to even dream of competing with the European powerhouses that had dominated the Vanderbilt Cup, a few, like Mike Boyle, were charging ahead with plans to obtain competitive machines. Others were taking a bolder approach, gambling that Yankee ingenuity could still play in the big leagues of motor sport. The Los Angeles basin was the center of a small but energetic collection of engineering geniuses and fabricators who refused to bow to the superiority of the Europeans and, wisely employing their limited funds, began to design and construct cars that could compete with the best at the Indianapolis Motor Speedway. Among them were former driver and car builder Lou Moore and technical wizards

Art Sparks and Ed Winfield, who, given the proper funding, could create powerful and reliable engines to rival the best in the world. Fred Offenhauser, Harry Miller's former chief engineer, operated a machine shop with a talented staff of technicians who were capable of creating first-class power plants, while brilliant fabricators, or "metal-men," like Curly Wetteroth, Herman Rigling, Myron Stevens, and Clyde Adams could create chassis and bodies of strength and beauty as if by magic.

It was into this cadre of brilliant men that a gangly, ambitious, but mildly eccentric Joel Wolfe Thorne, Jr. arrived in the mid-1930s. Possessing enormous wealth and consumed with a desire to dominate racing with his own cars and drivers, Thorne was the antithesis of streetwise tough guy Mike Boyle, having been raised with what in the day was derisively described as "a silver spoon in his mouth." It would be this brash young man, like none other, who would challenge Umbrella Mike for dominance at Indianapolis and as the most powerful figure in American motor sports.

Thorne used the firehouse technique, sloshing money around in appalling sums, gathering in its wake sports cars, whole racing teams, speedboats, airplanes, and dazzling women. In twenty hectic years Joel Thorne probably spent more, outraged more, upset more, and amused more than any other man in racing history. When things were going right, it was not uncommon for him to pull off an expensive sport coat and present it to its first admirer. But when his accounts were overdrawn, he lived like a bum, operating out of such unlikely hostelries as the coal bin of an Indianapolis hotel and subsisting from occasional bags of groceries dropped off by friends. Never a disciple of Dale Carnegie, he left dozens of associates gnashing their teeth in rage and frustration. At one point he borrowed one thousand dollars from a wealthy car owner. A few months later they quarreled and the owner demanded his money back. Joel waited until he was on the brink of arrest and then paid him off with a giant bagful of pennies.

If Joel possessed traits of character other than those normally associated with young millionaires, it might be said that he came by them honestly. His father, Joel Senior, sole heir to the massive fortune of Samuel and Phoebe Van Schoonhaven Thorne, was no Frank Merriwell himself. After nearly forty-five years of raising the eyebrows of New York society, Joel Senior married a little Irish girl named Mary Casey, a Barnard College professor who was thirteen years his junior. This betrothal was the final straw for his staid mother and father, and Joel and Mary found themselves cut off from the Thorne fortune in banking, railroading, importing, and Long Island real estate. But the birth of Joel Junior in 1914 thawed old Samuel visibly, and he doled out five hundred thousand dollars to help defer maternity costs and other expenses. When he died three years later, he left his grandson an outright grant of one million dollars.

By then Joel Senior and Mary had separated. Young Joel and his nurse were taken in by his grandmother, who was assisting his father in shrugging off his plebeian wife. The divorce trail was clogged with nastiness. Somehow the elder Joel and his mother managed to dredge up a sailor who testified to having less-than-honorable relations with Mary. She in turn opened the file on her husband, but, lacking the legal horsepower, the decision and custody of their son went to Joel Senior.

The mud from the trial had barely turned to dust when the younger Joel's grandmother died, leaving father and son alone with that stupendous pile of money. However, grandfather Samuel had spotted the seeds of impudence in his heir and before his death had tied the fortune into a labyrinth of trust funds and legacies. In the light of future events, it was a wise move. Not being inclined to settle down and assume the duties of full-time father, Joel Senior made arrangements to pasture his son in a good home. Mrs. Alice T. Sirkle of Denver, Colorado, got the job by answering a classified newspaper ad. For her efforts she received responsibility for young Joel and for the administration of his eighteen-thousand-dollar-a-year stipend.

In 1924 Joel Senior was clipped by a passing car while making repairs to his own vehicle along a Connecticut roadside. He died in a Danbury hospital. At ten years of age, his son has seen him but a few times in the past five years. The boy received his secondary education in relative peace and then came east to enter Rutgers University. He was reunited with his mother and moved her into a sixty-thousand-dollar spread near New Rochelle, New York.

Academically speaking, Joe (as he insisted on being

called, in preference to the more sedate-sounding Joel) was
an outstanding speedboat pilot. During his career at Rutgers he became known as the "Dizzy Dean of Outboards,"
and in 1933, at age nineteen, he won the American Out-
board Association High Point Trophy. In gathering 17,135
points to win the title, it was conservatively estimated that
Joe dumped fifty thousand dollars into the campaign.

After three years at Rutgers and a brief stay at the University of London, he gave up the cloistered life for more
exciting outlets—in the form of fast boats and cars and a
long, curvy file of stunning women. If anything fascinated
young Joe more than rakish, flame-belching machinery, it
was rakish, flame-belching women. With a wallet full of
money and an outlook on life that was something less
than monastic, he was able to keep himself well supplied
with superlative young ladies. As he began to infiltrate
the racing game, first as an interested spectator, then as a
fledging car owner and driver, he continually kept one of
these eye-popping females in tow. A worn personal biog-
raphy sheet still on file at the Indianapolis Motor Speedway serves as an excellent indication of how much Joe
enjoyed the opposite sex. After the query "Name your
greatest thrill at Indianapolis," he had neatly handwritten
one word—"Suzanna." Most old-timers at the speedway
can remember the days when Joe would import an array
of women from the West Coast each May, flying them in
first class. Invariably he would tire of their company after
a few giggly days and they would be returned home, by
Greyhound bus.

After 1934, automobile racing replaced speedboating as Thorne's second most important preoccupation. His formal entry into the upper echelons of the sport came as a car owner in the 1935 Indianapolis 500. As the sponsor of a ragged old Studebaker 8, driven by none other than newcomer Jimmy Snyder, Joe was almost unheralded in the racing world. The boys at Indy had seen rich kids arrive before, only to watch them scurry home when they sensed the frustration and drudgery of big-time automobile racing. The veterans were even more convinced they had seen the last of Thorne when his machine struggled home a dismal twenty-second. They were wrong. Joe would return in a fashion they would never forget. And in view of the future impact Joe's azure-hued cars would have at the Brickyard, there was an ironic aptness to the name of Snyder's 1935 car—the Blue Prelude Special.

Less than a month after the 1935 Indy 500, Joe took his first shot at driving. He chose to begin with a group with whom, on the surface at least, he seemed an ideal compatriot. The Automobile Racing Club of America (ARCA) was an organization devoted to the propagation of European-style road racing in the United States. In 1935 the ARCA was composed of a select coterie of well-to-do eastern sportsmen. To many of them, Indianapolis and its related track racing were a limbo inhabited by masses of slobbering, latter-day Visigoths. It was the habit of these gentlemen to hold discreet little speed fests on twisty, continental-type circuits in and near quiet hamlets like Alexandria Bay and Briarcliff, New York. In all justice to the

ARCA, the group fathered some outstanding racing talent, but they weren't prepared for Joe Thorne.

He made his entry at the "Grand Prix of the United States," scheduled for June 23, 1935, on the 3.29-mile Briarcliff course. He was among an exclusive starting group of seventeen men. While the field included imported Bugattis, Riley's, MGs, and racing Austins, Joe was at the wheel of a Ford roadster. No ordinary Ford, his car was a specially modified machine, built for the 1933 AAA Elgin Road Races, and was said to develop 120 bhp (brake horsepower) from its flathead V8 engine. It was generally acknowledged that the lippy twenty-one-year-old Thorne (at that time sporting a Ronald Coleman mustache) would be a genuine, if not entirely welcome, threat for top honors.

On the first lap of the ninety-nine-mile race, Thorne trundled the roadster from fifteenth to ninth place. Not a few of the gentlemen motorists, merely on the course for an afternoons' drive, were frightened silly as the Ford jounced out of the corners in full-lock slides. As the tight turns loomed, they watched in horror as Joe penetrated beyond all known shutoff markers before applying his tiny mechanical brakes. On occasion his Ford would exit up an escape road in a flurry of dust and stones as the less aggressive witnesses prudently rounded the corner, only to be sucked under again a few miles down the road.

Despite a number of diversionary trips, Joe managed to climb to third within five laps. At sixty-five miles he was in first place. But a pit stop dropped him to second, and he was unable to improve on that position before the checkered flag dropped. He equaled the lap record in his rush to catch up but finished 9.6 seconds astern Langdon Quimby's modified Willys 77.

After the race Joe created an unholy rumpus. Never one to mince words, he accused the race officials of blatantly cheating him out of the victory. Unused to this sort of nastiness, the ARCA accepted his protest without enthusiasm. After a perfunctory check of the lap charts, his complaint was flatly disallowed. There ended the short, fitful romance between Joe Thorne and amateur road racing.

The following year saw him back at the Indianapolis Motor Speedway with two cars powered by hulking six-cylinder Dodge engines (entered under the name of California relative Clifford Thorne because Joe was involved in a legal action at home). Experienced Russ Snowberger was assigned to one of them, while Joe planned to drive the twin. Difficulties began when Snowberger scraped off three feet of his car's nose on the retaining wall. In the meantime, Joe's driving convinced the AAA observers he was not yet ready for the 500 competition, and he relinquished his seat to veteran Dave Evans. But Evans couldn't get the car near qualifying speeds, and Joe left the track determined that 1937 would be different. That summer he entered a number of races to get seasoning for the Brickyard. Aside from lackluster performances on one-mile dirt tracks at Hammond, Indiana, Goshen, New York, and Springfield, Illinois, his only notable finish came at Pikes Peak. There he drove his dirt track Miller up the mountain to fourth place. During his training period, Joe courted a lovely Georgia-reared Powers model named Johnsie Eager and married her in November of that year.

At Indianapolis in early May 1937, Thorne met Art Sparks, a talented builder of race cars from Glendale, California. Sparks was a machine shop teacher at Glendale High School and had brought with him an automobile he had built that immediately caught Joe's eye. It was a long, narrow car with a 337-cubic-inch supercharged, straight-six DOHC engine that developed 500 bhp at 5,000 rpm on pump gasoline (which was required in 1937 at Indy). In a verbal agreement, Joe bought the car from Sparks. Jimmy Snyder was again given the driving assignment, and Chickie Hirashima, the Japanese American crew chief, was taken on as riding mechanic.

With one car in his stable, Joe toured the speedway's garage area—nicknamed "Gasoline Alley" after the popular newspaper cartoon strip—to buy more. The pits and garages buzzed about this towering kid who wrote spur-of-the-moment checks on napkins, bits of paper, and handkerchiefs for the equipment he wanted. As time trials approached, he had accumulated Floyd Roberts, Al Miller, and Floyd Davis with a trio of four-cylinder Millers; Zeke Meyer and an ancient Studebaker; Snyder and the Sparks; and for himself a 220 front-drive Offenhauser, more commonly referred to as an Offy.

Qualifications brought mixed blessings for Thorne. Emotions ranged from dizzy hilarity, when Snyder destroyed both the one- and ten-lap records during his time trial, to despair, when the boss himself turned in an official clocking of a mediocre 115.607 miles per hour. Roberts, Miller, and Davis made the race, but Meyer's Studebaker was an outright failure. When qualifying ended, Joe Thorne was the second alternate starter. Then first alternate, "Red" Schafer, withdrew, leaving him thirty-fourth. In a last-ditch effort to make the race, Joe had heard that another owner wanted to dump his Red Lion Special, which had been qualified by Cliff Bergere. Joe offered him five thousand dollars on the spot and the owner accepted. Joe immediately announced he was withdrawing the Red Lion Special and substituting his Offy in the lineup. Bergere, who found himself benched in the shuffle, was understandably peeved. The hassle was brought before track owner Eddie Rickenbacker and quickly resolved: Thorne could not switch cars.

"If you want to run in this race, you can damn well get out there and qualify like the rest of the drivers," Rickenbacker said to Joe.

"Keep up the tough talk, and I may buy the whole blasted starting field and watch you guys sweat on race day," snapped Joe.

"Try a stunt like that," cautioned Rickenbacker, who was one of the few men around nearly tall enough to look Joe square in the eyes, "and you'll run your next AAA race when you're ninety-seven," he said, according to *Car and Driver Magazine*.

His bluff thus called, Joe generously offered Bergere 25 percent of the winnings to drive for him (the going share for drivers was 35 to 40 percent). Bergere refused and Joe relented, granting him the standard split.

The race started with Joe sulking in the pits, that is until Snyder bellowed into the lead a few moments after the flag fell. He opened the gap with ease until the 28th lap, when a broken transmission put him out of the race. The rest of the Thorne team tried their best. Miller struggled through seven pit stops before retiring on the 170th circuit. Davis stopped five times before crashing on the 190th. Roberts, who would win the following year, nursed his car home in twelfth place. Bergere finished a creditable fifth, but it wasn't much help to Joe. His check had bounced (a standard Thorne failing), and the prize money and errant Red Lion Special were returned to the original owner.

Out of the tumult of 1937 one fact became clear to Joe: the Indianapolis 500 could not be overwhelmed by a massed frontal assault. Fast, quality machinery was needed. And in Art Sparks he figured he had just the man to supply him with the necessary equipment. After hiring Sparks, Joe spent the summer racing. He took a fifth at Pikes Peak and set the slowest qualifying time for the Syracuse, New York, one-hundred-miler run on the one-mile dirt oval at the New York State Fairgrounds. The high point of the season came with his old Alfa Romeo at the Vanderbilt Cup. A share of Joe's winnings gained in that memorable event, for being sixth overall and the second American to finish, helped to repair his supercharged 812 Cord convertible. He had been demonstrating the vehicle on the Roosevelt road course before the race and managed to bend it seriously during a wild spinout.

September 1, 1937, marked the beginning of the Thorne Engineering Company. On that date a giant warehouse on Slauson Avenue in Los Angeles was leased as a site to build racing cars. In the coming battle to win the Indianapolis 500, Joe's main opponent would be Mike Boyle, presuming Cotton Henning's mission to Italy bore fruit in the form of a proper Maserati.

5

TO BOLOGNA

COWS SCATTERED AND birds were flushed from nearby trees as the unmuffled engine crackled to life. Ernesto Maserati, his brow furrowed in concern, watched the young, swarthy engineer Guerino Bertocchi as he blipped the throttle, carefully warming the freshly minted three-liter, straight-eight power plant with its complex pair of twin super-chargers. When the engine reached proper operating temperature, Bertocchi nodded toward Ernesto and slipped the transmission into first gear, scouring the pave-ment and sending a fog of fine sand into the faces of Ernesto and the tiny cadre of mechanics left in his wake.

The run was taking place not at a racetrack, but on a long stretch of the Firenza Autostrada, reaching flat and true eastward toward the Adriatic Sea. It was a chill, sunny

January 20, 1938. As it was early in the morning, there was little traffic, save for an occasional farmer's truck chugging toward Bologna with a load of vegetables. Such tests were common in Italy, where motor racing was a national passion. Ordinary citizens, as well as the Fascist authorities, were more than happy to give way to the occasional race car that they believed might carry the crimson-red international colors of Italy to fame and glory.

Ernesto understood that any chance for the survival of his tiny company lay under the heavy foot of Bertocchi, his loyal and talented chief mechanic and one of the key men in the development of the new machine—soon to be known as the Maserati 8CTF. The unpainted, sleek single-seater was a pure racing car, unlicensed and bereft of even the most rudimentary road equipment such as headlights, wipers, roof, even doors. It would eventually be painted in Italy's international crimson-red racing colors, and it was a symphony of svelte shapes and contours. From its low snout and finely sculptured grillework to its swooping tail, it was as beautiful as it was fast. In an era long before aerodynamics and the raw laws of physics would create bizarre winged, four-wheeled monstrosities, the Maserati was as much kinetic artistry as it was a functional machine.

Deep in the leather seat behind the screeching engine, Bertocchi became as much a jockey as a driver, trying to control a man-made device that was, in its own way, as volatile and rebellious as a thoroughbred stallion. Like a great horse, it tolerated the man in its saddle, but only on its own terms, more than prepared to pitch him into the nearest ditch should he misbehave.

With the Maserati 8CTF lay Italy's hope in the intense world of International Grand Prix racing. To the north, over the Alps, the Nazi government of Hitler's Third Reich was pouring millions of reichsmarks into the support of highly advanced teams from Mercedes-Benz and the newly formed Auto Union, a Depression-based alliance of struggling automakers Audi, DKW, Wanderer, and Horch. Propaganda leader Joseph Goebbels understood the power of Germany's dominance in motor sport on the Continent, and his government's support had already produced amazing results, with their silver cars—known as *silber-feils*, or "silver arrows," producing over six hundred horsepower and capable of speeds on the open road in excess of two hundred miles an hour.

Ernesto and his two brothers, Bindo and Ettore, were taking a desperate gamble to compete against the power of the Nazi cars. Unlike the Hitler government, Benito Mussolini's Fascist regime in Rome was hardly as supportive. While much posturing and public acclamations were forthcoming, the poverty-stricken, struggling Fascists were devoting their limited financial resources to a futile campaign to develop a military force rivaling that of Germany.

The *Societa Anomina Officine Alfieri Maserati*, as the little Bologna-based operation was officially known, would have to struggle along, depending on its sales of racing cars to wealthy private customers, hand built in the former pottery factory on Bologna's Ponte Vecchio facing the ancient Roman Via Amelia. To the northwest, along the same stretch of road in the middle of the industrial city of Modena, entrepreneur and former racing driver Enzo Ferrari was in a similar situation, working with the Milanese auto manufacturer Alfa Romeo to run its racing operation through his privately operated Scuderia Ferrari.

Ernesto and his brothers would soon become neighbors—and archrivals—of Enzo Ferrari. The powerful Modenese Orsi family, led by Adolfo and his son Omer, had already invested in the Maserati firm and were about to move the operation to a large and elaborate factory on the Via Menotti in Modena. Their plan was not only to exploit the little firm's spark plug business, but also to continue building race cars on a limited basis. But moving to Modena lay in the future, and Ernesto now concentrated his considerable talents on the development of the 8CTF, one final and desperate attempt to retain Italian honor and pride in the face of the German onslaught.

Bertocchi was at the wheel of the three brothers' prototype 8CTF, chassis 3030. Like all the Maserati racing machines that had been constructed in limited numbers since the firm had been created in 1926, it was as much a rolling sculpture as it was a racing automobile. Like many northern Italian cities, Bologna was a center of foundries, metalworking artisans, and craftsmen whose traditions were linked to the Renaissance. Aesthetics was as important as function, and chassis 3030, like all of the cars created by the Maserati brothers, was a masterpiece in metal.

Its polished engine block, gearbox, and differential all had the factory's Neptune-based trident emblem cast in the glistening alloys.

The family had been involved with high-performance automobiles since Carlo, the oldest of seven brothers born to Rodolfo and Carolina Maserati between 1881 and 1894, began racing for the tiny Bianchi firm in 1907. The first car to bear the Maserati trident appeared in the Targa Florio open road race in Sicily on April 25, 1926. The car was driven by thirty-nine-year-old Alfieri, the most talented behind the wheel of the family. Badly injured in a crash while running the Coppa Messina race in May 1927, Alfieri continued to lead the little firm until his premature death in March 1932. By then the three remaining brothers (the others had died or left the business), led by Ernesto, who was a brilliant engineer and a superb driver, had expanded to the manufacture of high-performance spark plugs in addition to the creation of hand-built racing machines. With Italy immersed in the disastrous Ethiopian war, and Benito Mussolini obsessed with the absurd notion of reviving the Roman Empire, the tiny Maserati operation struggled onward with the three brothers living above the Ponte Vecchio factory and laboring daily to remain in international motor sports. Despite their lack of funds, the cars they laboriously fabricated were competitive even in faraway America.

In 1930 the first Maserati appeared at the Indianapolis 500. Factory driver Baconin Borzacchini started twenty-eighth in a sixteen-cylinder car and lasted only seven laps before a magneto failure. Privateer Letterio Cuccinotta did better in his eight-cylinder model, starting thirtieth but finishing twelfth. It was an inauspicious beginning for a firm that within a decade would dominate the great race.

The car that Bertocchi tested in January 1938 was the first of three 8CTFs built by the brothers during that year. Compared to the multimillion-dollar reichsmark campaigns by Mercedes-Benz and Auto Union, or even the Fascist government-supported cars being created by rival Alfa Romeo, the 8CTFs were feeble efforts, based essentially on existing components. Rather than creating a new engine, the brothers had merely grafted two older four-cylinder, 1.5-liter 4CM engine blocks on a common crankcase and cylinder head to create a straight-eight. The chassis, while exquisite in terms of craftsmanship, carried a relatively modern independent front suspension but an archaic solid rear axle sprung by half-elliptic, wagon-style leaf springs.

Finally completed in March 1938, two Maserati 8CTFs, chassis 3030 and 3031, appeared at the Tripoli Grand Prix run on the 8.14-mile Mellaha circuit in Italy's African colony. In the hands of sports car ace Felice Trossi, who had funded his own car, 8CTF 3031 amazed the German teams by turning in the fastest practice time, 136 miles per hour, but broke its transmission in the race after leading for eleven laps. Mercedes-Benz went on to win the top three places, but it nevertheless was an impressive debut for the Maserati. Achille Varzi, another Italian ace, who also paid for the construction of his sister car, chassis 3031, also lost its transmission. The two cars reappeared that summer in Italy at Livorno and Pescara, where Luigi Villoresi again set the fastest lap in 3031 before retiring with magneto problems.

It was September before the third 8CTF, chassis 3032, was to be completed and driven by Calabrian native Goffredo "Freddie" Zehender at the Italian Grand Prix held at the Monza circuit on the outskirts of Milan. Early in the race Zehender stuffed the new car on top of a concrete barrier bordering the track and retired the best machine. Villoresi then broke a supercharger drive in 3030 early in the race, while Felice Trossi soldiered 3031 on to a fifth-place finish, only to be disqualified for being assisted by spectators when his car stalled mid-race. The final outing for the 8CTFs in 1938 was an entry by Villoresi in 3030 at the Donnington Grand Prix on October 22. For reasons unknown, the brothers were late arriving at the track and Villoresi had no chance to practice. He started last and was never a factor in the race, finishing far behind the winner, Tazio Nuvolari, who drove a factory-made Auto Union.

Stunted by endemic financial shortages and no support from the Mussolini government, the Maserati brothers, with supporters Zehender, Trossi, and Varzi, parked the three 8CTFs for the remainder of the 1938 season and waited either to sell them to private customers or to generate an infusion of cash from the Orsis. However, the new Modenese investors were primarily interested in the Maserati spark plug business rather than the race cars and offered little prospect for major funding for a serious campaign during the 1939 Grand Prix season.

Moreover, war clouds were gathering across Europe at a shocking rate. In March Adolf Hitler seized Austria. This outraged the French and British governments but generated no response other than Prime Minister Neville Chamberlain's "appeasement" policy and a widely publicized statement by American air hero Charles Lindbergh that Great Britain could not possibly win a war in Europe against the Germans, even with American help. Meanwhile, the savage assaults on the Jewish populations in Russia, Germany, and Italy steadily intensified.

Lindbergh's rantings about American isolationism from the European conflict gained resonance, especially in the Midwest, where plans for the traditional Memorial Day five-hundred-mile race at Indianapolis proceeded as if Nazism, Communism, and Fascism were on another planet. By January 1939, through a series of letters and cables, Mike Boyle and Cotton Henning had reached an agreement with the Maserati brothers to obtain chassis 3032, the last of the three 8CTFs that had been built the year before and had performed in the inept hands of Freddie Zehender. This time Henning would make the trip to Bologna himself to make sure the machine would be the proper size and not another midget like the 6CM. It was part of the negotiation that the little car would be returned to the factory in partial trade for the larger and more effective version that, according to the Maserati brothers, would be available.

All the pieces seemed to be in place until February 8, 1939. On that rainy night in Indianapolis Boyle team member Wild Bill Cummings was retuning home from his Lucky-7 bar when his Cadillac skidded on the wet pavement and slammed against a concrete bridge abutment. Gravely injured, he lingered for four days in a coma before word spread across the nation that the great champion was dead.

Over the past few years, two men besides the now-deceased Cummings had dominated the 500. Californian Louis "Louie" Meyer had won the race three times—in 1928, 1933, and 1936—and was known not only as an affable, expert driver but also as a brilliant mechanic who had helped build his two most recent winning cars. Meyer had made his first appearance at Indianapolis Motor Speedway in 1927, ironically as the mechanic for none other than Wilbur Shaw. When Shaw suffered exhaustion at the wheel of his Jynx Special during mid-race, novice Meyer had climbed aboard and drove for forty-one laps, holding Shaw's position. His first victory in the 500 came a year later, and his second came in 1933, when his riding mechanic was his personal physician, Dr. Lawson Harris, nicknamed "Useless" by his friends. After his third victory, in 1936, Meyer joined the Boyle team in 1937, driving the car that Bill Cummings had ridden to victory four years earlier, and finished fourth. While he, Cummings, and Henning were good friends, Meyer abandoned the Boyle operation a year later to join master engine and car builders Bud and Ed Winfield in creating his own car, backed by Bowes Seal Fast.

That left defending 500 champion Wilbur Shaw as the only major candidate for the Boyle Maserati. Shaw's experience with the Fiermonte 8VRi at the 1936 Vanderbilt Cup

had convinced him of the Maserati brothers' potential
for building a winning car for Indianapolis. Moreover, his
"pay car," which had carried him to victory in May of that
year, was designed as a two-man machine with a wide body
that was now obsolete against the smaller, lighter, leaner
cars allowed in the coming years. Even if Shaw understood that he might be forced to remain with his own
automobile for another season because of the delay in
obtaining a new machine from Europe, he was savvy
enough to believe that the wait could reap large rewards
in the future. Such was the potential for victory carried in
the advanced machinery being designed and built by the
European factories. Against that technology, the tiny, marginally bankrupt independent racing shops operating in
America with no help from the domestic auto industry
faced certain doom when and if the foreigners decided to
make a major assault on the world's greatest race.

While struggling with the Fiermonte Maserati at the
1937 Vanderbilt race, Shaw became convinced that if he
could obtain one of the newer, more advanced, Italian-
built race cars like a Maserati or the Alfa Romeo that
friendly rival Rex Mays had driven to third place, he could
dominate the Indianapolis 500. The day before the Vanderbilt, Shaw was sitting with some friends in front of his
garage when one of the new Maseratis was pushed past by
its crew.

"If I had a car like that, I'd win Indy," he said.

Mike Boyle overheard the remark and responded, "If I
can get you one, will you drive it?"

"I will if it's half as fast as I think it is," replied Shaw. "I wouldn't want to give up my pay car for something that isn't as good, but if I don't like the Maserati, I'll get a good man to drive it for you," he added.

"You've got a deal," said Mike Boyle. "Cotton Henning is headed to Italy to negotiate with the Maserati brothers in a few weeks."

After further negotiation at Henning's residence at the downtown Indianapolis Antlers Hotel, Shaw was given the assignment to drive the new car, presuming it was the potent machine that Henning believed was being constructed in Bologna. The brothers had assured Henning that such a car would be for sale, but rather than being snookered twice, Boyle agreed to send Henning to Bologna to see for himself. He left his Indianapolis home on March 2, 1939, driving to New York in Boyle's flatbed Ford truck. Embarking on the Italian liner *Comte di Savoia*, he landed in Genoa and took a train to Bologna, where he was introduced to chassis 3032, which had been repaired after the Zehender crash. The price would be fifteen thousand U.S. dollars—about three hundred thousand dollars in today's dollars—and roughly double the cost of the Indy machines being built by American craftsmen.

This would clearly be the only way that the team could obtain a proper Grand Prix machine from the brothers, who, for reasons unknown, seemed unable to make a sale without a face-to-face confrontation. If Mike Boyle was to gain access to one of the only advanced Grand Prix cars available, there was no choice but to send Cotton Henning on the journey not only to a strange land, but to a nation that was now embroiled in the wild politics of Fascism promoted and dominated by a former Milanese journalist named Benito Mussolini.

Having seized power in 1922, the strutting, pugnacious little man was determined to revive Italy to the past glories of the Roman Empire—a mad notion considering his country's feeble economy and impoverished population. Operating in the shadow of the ruthless Adolf Hitler, who had transformed Germany into a dangerous, highly mechanized military machine, Mussolini was only able to create the trappings of strength through lavish parades, elegant uniforms, and enormous rallies. But behind such facades he led an army that had barely been able to defeat a primitive, spear-carrying band of Ethiopian natives during a farcical invasion of that backwater African nation.

After exchanging cables with Boyle, in which Henning positively evaluated the machine, the purchase was cleared and shipment began via freighter to New York. A little more than a month was left before practice opened at the Indianapolis Motor Speedway. Boyle also authorized Henning to purchase a spare engine and extra parts for the car, although the brothers warned that it might take nearly a month before another exotic three-liter power plant could be fabricated and shipped to America. Encouraged by the results of his trip, Henning returned to New York by ship and waited in a Manhattan hotel for the Maserati to arrive. Shaw flew commercially to LaGuardia airport and eagerly took up residence with Henning to await the car, which had now become news to the local sporting press and to racing enthusiasts in the metropolitan area.

The April 21, 1939, issue of *Illustrated Speedway News,* published in Brooklyn, produced an exclusive front-page photo of the Maserati being unloaded at a Newark, New Jersey, dock, carefully (or so it seemed) wrapped in burlap for the Atlantic voyage. Standing with Henning in the photo was Ralph De Palma, the famous retired driving champion, and Ira Vail, a prominent East Coast race promoter. The caption described the car as a "thunderbug imported speed creation to be driven by Wilbur Shaw in the coming Indianapolis classic."

After loading the car on Boyle's Ford flatbed truck, Henning and Shaw headed west toward Indianapolis. Rolling down a steep hill in western Pennsylvania, the gasoline tank on the aging Ford shook loose, causing a moment of panic and frantic roadside repairs by the two skilled mechanics. The pair stood in vivid contrast to passing motorists. Diminutive Shaw appeared childlike in the shadow of Henning, a man with thinning blond hair whose girth had increased concurrently with his success in maintaining Boyle's racing cars. If nothing else, Mike Boyle was a generous employer, and Henning had long since left his backwater Missouri roots to become a prosperous, if not wealthy, leader in the tight and exclusive community of world-class motor sports mechanics. Despite their diverse physical architectures, Shaw and Henning were close friends, sharing both strong, conservative Midwestern values and an intense passion for high-powered automobiles.

But the brief breakdown was only a modest prelude to the trouble that awaited them when they arrived at Henning's shop in Indianapolis. It was Shaw who first spotted a pool of water under the Maserati's aluminum belly pan on the wooden bed of the truck. Scores of race fans, local newsmen, and other race team members were clustered around the truck waiting for the new machine to be unloaded. Shaw quickly had Henning clear the shop and close the doors as they privately unloaded the automobile in search of what surely had to be a leak. The discovery could not have been more troubling. The Maserati mechanics had fired up the car's engine for Henning before preparing it for shipment to America. But they had apparently forgotten—or did not bother—to drain the radiator and engine of the water they had employed as coolant. Either during the Atlantic crossing or on the chilly trip through the Pennsylvania mountains, the water had frozen, rupturing both four-cylinder blocks that had been joined to create the 8CTF's engine.

Remaining silent and pledging secrecy, even to Mike Boyle—who, because of his endless legal and union battles in Chicago, was not present—Shaw and Henning sought a solution. Welding the cracks in the aluminum was impossible. There being no replacements in America, a frantic cable was sent to the Maserati brothers requesting immediate shipment of the already-purchased spare engine, numbered 3033, initially intended for the next 8CTF to be built (which never happened). Although the Maserati brothers' efficiency levels were hindered by their move from Bologna to Modena, they still responded quickly. Despite the rising conflict in Europe and Italy's increased war footing, the brothers somehow managed to get the engine to New York within three weeks by rail and Pan Am transatlantic clipper. From there Henning engaged a local trucking company to haul the engine to Indianapolis, where, within hours, he and Shaw installed it in the 8CTF's engine bay.

Clearly the Maserati brothers saw the opportunity to save their reputation, and perhaps their company, by winning the Indianapolis 500 in faraway America. Believing the Italian American population would celebrate such a victory, the brothers tried their best, with limited funds and personnel, to support Boyle and Shaw in the best way possible if for no other reason than for their own salvation.

It was now time to contact Mike Boyle to introduce him to the new machine. The question remains: was it his car or Henning's? Although it was surely Boyle's money that purchased the automobile and spare engine, it may have been that for tax purposes and other legal entanglements haunting Umbrella Mike, the actual ownership of the vehicle was Henning's. No matter what was in the paper agreement, there is no question that major funding for the car came from Boyle's ever-expanding bank account, built on the power and influence of his Chicago IBEW Local 134. Surely with the hard-edged connections Boyle had with the city's mobsters, Henning understood that any abuse of his "ownership" might have deadly consequences.

Since the Roaring Twenties, when Mike Boyle began bringing cars to Indianapolis—a total of twenty up to

1939—the entrants' names had constantly changed for reasons that were unknown but probably linked to his fluctuating legal battles. Until 1932 the cars had carried the Boyle Valve logo on their cowls and were entered either by his primary driver, Cliff Woodbury, or by the Boyle Valve Company, which manufactured high-quality engine valves for both passenger and racing machines. By 1933 Boyle's cars were entered by "M. J. Boyle" and sponsored by "Boyle Products." Cotton Henning became an entrant under the name "H. C. Henning" in 1934 along with such entities as "Boyle Products," "Boyle Racing Headquarters," and "Boyle Motor Products." In 1938 three of Boyle's cars carried the IBEW union sponsorship, although in all cases either Boyle or Henning actually owned the machines in a mysterious contractual agreement that, in the end, involved funding by the union boss.

Once the new engine was bolted in place, Henning shoved a hand crank into the snout of the car and with a quarter turn all eight cylinders thundered awake. The acrid fumes of the methanol fuel recommended by the factory filled the small space, bringing smiles and tears to the two men's eyes before Henning revved the engine one last time and switched off the ignition. It was now time to call Umbrella Mike and show him the new creation. Shaw telephoned his boss, telling him that if he could make it by the next afternoon, he and Henning would meet him at the Indianapolis Motor Speedway, where he would take the car for a few practice laps. Boyle agreed, and by late morning the next day, Boyle, in company with two silent, stern-faced men with bulges in their suit jackets, appeared at the speedway's Gasoline Alley. After examining the crimson-bodied machine, Boyle turned to Henning and said, "Let me hear her run."

Henning yanked hard on the crank. Nothing. Another hard twist. Nothing. More increasingly urgent cranks, but the big Maserati remained a sleepless giant. All afternoon Henning and Shaw fiddled with the engine, checking every possible electrical and fuel connection without success. As the sun began to set, Umbrella Mike, his Irish face dark with anger, stalked out of the garage and growled, "If you ever get that thing running, give me a ring."

Rather than drive the 185 miles back to Chicago and his elegant home at 304 Grand Boulevard with his wife, Minnie, and their two sons—who were also involved in the electrical union—Boyle took a suite at the Claypool Hotel in downtown Indianapolis. At fifty-nine years, he had long since lost his lyrical Irish sense of humor. His business life was intense, with the FBI and other government agencies examining his every move, always threatening more indictments and arrests. His racing efforts appeared to be a legitimate pastime, although opportunities for money laundering had significant potential, both for him personally and for the union as a whole.

Henning and Shaw understood that they were not dealing with one of the wealthy gentlemen sportsmen who generally entered cars at Indianapolis, even in the Depression-haunted 1930s. Mike Boyle, always given a wide berth by the sporting press, which vaguely described

him merely as a "union leader," had the kind of connections that simple racing drivers and mechanics did not
tamper with. But thanks to his obscure and deep sources
of funding, Shaw and Henning were in a position to win
the great Indianapolis race with a unique and powerful
automobile obtained only through the involvement of a
man with a dark and ominous past.

Not only did the press give Umbrella Mike a free pass
regarding his racing involvement, but so did the officials
at the Indianapolis Motor Speedway as well as the American Automobile Association Contest Board members, who
sanctioned the 500. Although they surely knew about
Boyle's gangland connections, he was to them just another
wealthy car owner, who ultimately was able to attract fans—
and revenue—to a sport hard hit by the sagging national
economy. Eddie Rickenbacker, who ran the speedway with
an iron hand, no doubt looked the other way when impli-
cations were mentioned regarding Umbrella Mike's shady
business dealings and his links with both the Italian and
Irish mobs who controlled Chicago. Why dabble with such
issues when Boyle was the source of big money that benefited the struggling business of big-time motor racing?

Baffled by the new Maserati engine's failure to start in
the presence of Boyle, Henning and Shaw left the car and
went to the Antlers Hotel, where over drinks and dinner
they tried to determine the source of the trouble. After
completing a mental checklist, Henning realized they had
examined everything in the engine except for the spark
plugs. For all intents and purposes they seemed to be in

perfect shape. No matter, they decided, another look was required.

The next morning they returned to the inert machine, and as a last resort, Henning pulled out eight fresh Maserati-manufactured spark plugs from the mass of spares sent by the brothers and screwed them into the engine. The brutish power plant came to life with half a twist of the crank. A call was made to Boyle to meet them within an hour. Again the engine behaved perfectly.

A short test drive at the speedway revealed that the front wheels wobbled at low speeds, perhaps as a result of the Zehender crash. But after balancing them with no improvements, Henning found the long steering arms flexed in the sweeping corners. Unable to fabricate a replacement at such a late date, he stiffened the units with specially carved lengths of hardwood hickory, a primitive but effective cure to the ailment.

Umbrella Mike had arrived at the track still in company with the two anonymous thugs. Henning and Shaw greeted him along pit row with Shaw already wearing his helmet and goggles and ready for a test drive. Daring to play a joke on Boyle, Henning cranked the engine. Again, nothing happened. With Boyle about to growl, Henning grabbed a wrench and deftly installed eight fresh plugs. The engine instantly fired, bringing a smile to Boyle's broad Irish face.

Shaw eased into the cockpit. Sitting deep in the leather seat, barely able to see over the cowling and having to tip-toe to reach the throttle—which in European racing style was placed between the clutch and brake—Shaw still found the Maserati to his liking. With the drainpipe-sized, chrome-plated exhaust at his left elbow thumping with the special resonance reserved only for straight-eight, unmuffled engines and the clatter and whine of the gear train issuing from the long louvered hood that led him around the speedway, Shaw immediately felt linked to the great machine, as if he had saddled up on a balky but essentially friendly racehorse, ready at his whim to gallop at astounding velocities when given its head.

Like the millennium-old link between man and horse, that between man and machine could be unpredictable and sometimes dangerous. But when a symbiosis between the horse and rider or car and driver was created, amazing results lay ahead. Such was the bonding between Shaw and the Maserati from the first moment he aimed the big red wagon into the speedway's sweeping, quarter-mile-long first turn. Understanding that Henning could easily adjust the seat and pedals to accommodate his small frame, Shaw fell in love quickly, finding the so-called groove for maximum speed. He ran four quick laps, which Henning's stopwatch recorded at 127 miles per hour. This was two miles an hour quicker than the top qualifying speed of the 1938 500 winner, Floyd Roberts, and seemed to place the Maserati firmly among the fastest contenders for the upcoming race.

Openly pleased with the results, Boyle climbed into the backseat of his armored Cadillac sedan and headed back to his elaborate suite at the Claypool. There began a party that lasted throughout the night, with revelers including his

Wilbur Shaw's movie star good looks helped him become a major American celebrity in the late 1930s. (Kirkpatrick Photo, IMS)

Joe Thorne
Indianapolis Motor Speedway 1939.

"Umbrella Mike" Boyle (left) *with Cotton Henning, spent millions of his Electrical Union's funds to field top-flight drivers, crews, and automobiles for the Indianapolis 500. (Kirkpatrick Photo, IMS)*

The Boyle racing team traveled first class during the Depression. (Kirkpatrick Photo, IMS)

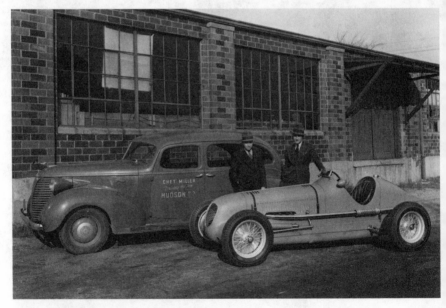

Mike Boyle was among the first American racing car owners to identify the potential of European Grand Prix cars like the Italian-built Maseratis. (Kirkpatrick Photo, IMS)

Wilbur Shaw instantly found Boyle's 8CTF Maserati to his liking during practice for the 1939 Indianapolis 500. (Dick Wallen Productions)

Shaw's first Indianapolis 500 win with the Boyle Maserati in May 1939, was his second visit to the Speedway's victory lane, having already won the big race in 1937. (Dick Wallen Productions)

Wilbur Shaw is mobbed in victory lane following his third "500" victory in May 1940—and the second straight with Mike Boyle's Maserati. (Indy 500 Photos, IMSC)

Jimmy Snyder seated beside the car, was the fastest man at Indianapolis in the late 1940s at the wheel of Joel Thorne's superb Thorne Engineering Special. The car is being checked for wheel alignment in the Speedway's "Gasoline Alley" prior to the 1939 500. (Kirkpatrick Photo, IMS)

Wilbur Shaw—retired and running the Speedway in May 1946, aboard a two-man Schwinn bicycle with rising star Ted Horn. The Speedway's famed "Pagoda" timing tower is in the background. (Kirkpatrick Photo, IMS)

The front row starting lineup from the 1947 Indianapolis 500. Ted Horn (left) is on the "pole position" with the ex-Boyle/Shaw Maserati then owned by the Bennett Brothers. In the middle is Cliff Bergere in the potent Novi V8 with race winner Mauri Rose on the outside in the new Lou Moore front-drive Blue Crown Spark Plug Special. Horn was to finish third while Bergere ended up 21st with mechanical troubles. (Kirkpatrick Photo, IMS)

Wilbur Shaw's first exposure to a Maserati came at the 1937 Vanderbilt Cup road race on New York's Long Island. A broken exhaust pipe dropped him out of contention, but convinced him that a properly prepared European Grand Prix car could win the Indianapolis 500. (Smith Hempstone Oliver collection)

union buddies and thugs from Chicago; local friends; a bevy of imported, high-priced hookers; and enough booze—much of it illegally imported from Canada—to, in the argot of the day, "float a battleship." Henning and Shaw stayed for part of the evening, but neither was a heavy drinker and both felt uncomfortable among Boyle's crowd. However, they were the stars of the evening, having made headlines across the nation, thanks to a massive Associated Press story that chronicled Shaw's record run. Pummeled by handshakes and backslaps from the Boyle bunch, the two men politely took leave before nine o'clock, explaining that further preparations on the car were necessary, but failing to discuss with Boyle or anyone else that despite the Maserati's superb performance, there were mysteries in the engine that might pose real problems during the upcoming race.

On the way home from the party, Shaw and Henning puzzled why the car continued to behave so crankily without fresh spark plugs. If during the race the engine stopped while in a pit stop, installing fresh plugs would result in the loss of precious minutes. Close examination revealed that a microscopic film was forming on the plug's electrodes when the engine was stopped, blocking the spark that ignited the fuel. A series of cables to the Maserati factory revealed that this happened only when methanol alcohol was employed, not when regular gasoline was in the tank. Still baffled about the exact chemistry in play, Henning installed a small tank of gasoline in the firewall of the Maserati. In that way the system could be switched from methanol to gasoline for a few moments before the engine was stopped, thereby cleaning the plugs. Henning's idea was to remain an essential, if secret, component of the Maserati's engine for the life of the car.

As Shaw continued to test the car before the formal qualifying runs for the five-hundred-mile race, a leak was discovered in the engine's rear main bearing. Knowing that a repair would require days of disassembling and reassembling the complex engine, Henning instead installed a six-gallon auxiliary oil tank under the driver's bucket seat. Speedway rules forbade adding engine oil during the race, and rather than risking the engine running dry, the extra lubricant seemed to guarantee that the Maserati could run the distance. The fact that oil dribbling from the leaky bearing during the race could possibly lead to a wreck if another automobile followed too closely did not seem to concern either Henning or Shaw.

With the Maserati patched up with the two extra tanks for gasoline and oil, the little team was supremely confident that they could run with the best of the competition. But aware of some reported engine and transmission failures in Europe, Henning made several modifications to increase reliability. Although the Maseratis claimed 365 horsepower for their engine, he was worried about the weak, three-main-bearing engine being able to last five hundred miles, so he readjusted the twin superchargers to cut output to a less stressful 350 horsepower. He also fitted the car with larger nineteen-inch wire wheels and Firestone tires (in place of the original Pirellis) in order to sustain higher speeds with lower engine rpms (about 5,800 or

500 rpm below the so-called red-line limit) and to employ tires that were specially designed for the giant speedway.

The Maserati 8CTF, chassis 3032, but with engine 3033, was repainted a deep, burgundy red with cream-colored number 2s on its long hood. This was Shaw's assigned AAA number based on his 1938 finish in the national championship. On the cowl was emblazoned "Boyle Special" with a long-stemmed Irish clay pipe and a tiny, green three-leafed-clover on the bowl. In this elegant motif the Boyle Special Maserati was ready for the five-hundred-mile race that lay ahead.

Others who were arriving for practice were convinced that they packed the power and the talent to beat back the new threat from Italy. Mike Boyle's new super car from Italy, although flashy and intriguing, hardly frightened Shaw's major rivals at the speedway, who had also arrived from California with machines they considered more than capable of beating back the "foreign invader." Southern California was a hotbed of high-performance engineering, and a pack of race car fabricators, engine builders, engineers, and wealthy sportsmen based there were more than prepared to face the new challenge posed by Umbrella Mike and Wee Wilbur Shaw.

6

THE RACE TEAMS FORM

AS THE SPRING of 1938 blossomed in the placid Midwest, cities like Indianapolis, Indiana, seemed to occupy another planet separated from the madness rising in Europe and the Far East. The local newspapers reported Hitler's continued persecution of the Jews and Stalin's savage purges, while the Spanish Civil War raged and the Japanese continued their invasion of mainland China. But more important issues distracted the Hoosiers as the nation remained saddled with 5.8 million people unemployed. Eddie Rickenbacker, owner of the great local motor speedway, announced that he and partner Lawrence Rockfeller had purchased the struggling North American Aviation Company for $3.5 million and would create Eastern Airlines. This prompted many Indianapolis businessmen and journalists to question whether the famed aviator was planning to either sell or close the speedway that meant so much to the area's economy each May.

As the American automobile industry in Detroit struggled with sagging sales and increasing unrest between management and the powerful United Auto Workers Union, word was received that Hitler was about to open a giant plant in Wolfsburg that would manufacture a "people's car" called the Volkswagen. This only amplified fears that the rising economic and military power of the Third Reich would somehow soon threaten even faraway America. After all, the raging dictator had blatantly seized neighboring Austria in March, while France and Great Britain had stood by in silence as British Prime Minister Neville Chamberlain nattered about "peace in our time."

Powerful, opposing social and political forces were in play across America. As the nation crawled out of the Great Depression, helped by government programs created by Roosevelt's New Deal, the division between the rich and the poor remained deep and seemingly insolvable. Into this rift came the Communist and Nazi parties, both of which gained brief but vivid power in New York, Chicago, and other major cities. Meanwhile, the labor unions—some of which were strongly linked to the hard left-wing cores of the Socialist and Communist movements—were wresting power from the moguls who controlled such major industries as steel, coal, and Detroit's automobile business.

As Hitler and Mussolini built up massive military power and threatened all of Western Europe, Stalin and his thugs engaged in hidden atrocities, sending millions to their deaths in Siberian concentration camps. In the Far East, Imperial Japan was murdering its way across China while the two great Western powers—Great Britain and the United States—looked the other way. And as Chamberlain rhapsodized about "peace in our time," the Germans chuckled behind his back. Across the United States and in Washington, the so-called Isolationists preached a policy that would keep America out of "foreign wars" thanks to the twin barriers of the Atlantic and Pacific Oceans. This lunacy would maintain major support among the American citizenry until they woke to the news of Pearl Harbor on Sunday, December 7, 1941.

When practice opened for the 500 in early May 1938, Hoosiers were fascinated with the new game of Bingo, and teenage bobby-soxers in faddish new saddle shoes danced to the swing music of Glenn Miller and Benny Goodman and read the new comic strip *Superman,* created by Cleveland cartoonists Jerry Siegel and Joe Schuster. A young, undersized racehorse named Seabiscuit was winning races, and sports writers everywhere predicted that before the year ended a match race would be set up between the newcomer and the predominant stallion of the day, War Admiral.

It was clear that Umbrella Mike and Joel Wolfe Thorne were headed for an ugly head-butting rivalry in search of domination at Indianapolis. They were almost universal opposites in every possible social and economic aspect of modern life. Boyle was Irish to the core, being born of immigrants who, like millions of their countrymen, had fled the Auld Sod after the terrible potato famine of 1845 that had killed more than 2.5 million people from Dublin to Moscow and shattered the Irish economy for decades. His background was purely Roman Catholic, lower-middle class, with proud links to the early labor union movements and experiments in socialism and Marxism by Robert La Follette and others that ruffled the business establishment and the upper classes at the end of the nineteenth century.

Although Joel Wolfe Thorne insisted on being called Joe by his racing peers and tried to behave like a "real guy," his patrician background was never well concealed. An heir to the Manufacturer's Hanover banking fortune, he often feigned poverty but was never more than a checkbook away from his family's millions, which had left him with a perpetual open door to the highest echelons of his society. Joe Thorne was a one-off in motor sport, as his antics while running with gentlemen amateurs in various sports car races on the East Coast had infuriated his peers, driving as he did like a madman and dressing like a hobo. The gawky six-footer liked nothing better than to outrage his high society friends by behaving like a barbarian while running through a series of beautiful women.

Boyle and Thorne had both come to Indianapolis in 1938 with three cars in their stables. Boyle's collection included Rose's little 6CM Maserati mistakenly sent from Italy plus Bill Cummings in his rebodied Miller and young charger Chet Miller (no relation to Harry) in another, aged Miller. All three cars were ostensibly entered with sponsorship by the IBEW in the name of Boyle Racing Headquarters. During his twenty-year campaign in major league auto racing, it had apparently never entered Mike Boyle's mind to build his own cars, as he found it more effective to buy those already constructed by others—especially by such respected experts as the Maserati brothers, who, during the running of the 1938 500, were busily designing and building the three 8CTFs that, ironically, would all end up in the Hoosier heartland.

Purchasing someone else's castoffs was hardly Joe Thorne's game. Not only did he have vastly more funds than Boyle, but he fancied himself something of an engineer with talent to create an American-built car that would overwhelm the European imports favored by Boyle and others. To run the newly formed Thorne Engineering Company, Art Sparks had been signed to a lifetime contract. He was to receive two hundred dollars per month plus expenses, one hundred thousand dollars in life and health insurance until age seventy-five, 10 percent of all speedway winnings, 15 percent of all other prize money, and 5 percent of the company's gross profits. Not bad for a start.

Joe spent $125,000 outfitting the midtown Los Angeles shop on Slauson Avenue. Complete facilities for pattern making, tooling, machinery, and testing were installed. To keep close to the operation, Joe had an apartment built on the roof. The quarters had a large picture window that looked down into the shop so that he could relax by the fire and watch his cars take shape.

"This was the kind of extravaganza that made Joe look like a complete nut," said an old racing associate. "But don't for one minute think he didn't know what he was doing. He had the idea that his money would buy anything, while at the same time it excluded him from following the rules. Joe honestly didn't give a hoot what most people thought of him, and he acted accordingly."

The Thorne Engineering plan was to build a pair of three-liter, supercharged straight-sixes to conform to the 1938 FIA (Fédération Internationale de l'Automobile) Formula. To implement this, Sparks rounded up some of the top mechanical talent in racing. Joe Petrali and Eddie Offut were hired as foremen, and Clyde Adams came on to do the bodywork. In all, eighteen men worked the day shift, and nine more labored through the night. Two draftsmen and a pair of office helpers rounded out the staff.

With the magnesium cylinder blocks cast by Dow Chemical, the engines were ready for testing in seven months. They easily cranked out 365 bhp at 6,500 rpm. Powering 105-inch-wheelbase cars weighing 1,845 pounds dry, the "Big Sixes" were truly classic milestones in the development of speedway equipment. The driveshafts were mounted to the left of the driver, thus lowering the center of gravity and predating the roadster designs that dominated Indianapolis in the 1950s and early 1960s.

Joe wisely decided that his limited experience precluded an immediate leap into his new toys. Jimmy Snyder was again hired to drive one of them, and all-time midget-racing great Ronnie Householder got the other. Joe entered his old 220 Offy, and a second four-banger was assigned to Billy DeVore. Snyder and Householder quickly found that the new cars would go like sin. Both were clocked through Bud Winfield's unofficial speed trap on the Indianapolis back stretch at over 174 miles per hour.

Exactly how much inspiration came from Joe's friendly inducement to "qualify faster than I do or you're fired" is not known, but Householder set an absolute ten-lap qualifying record at 125.769 miles per hour (which still stands because the speedway adopted the four-lap trial the following year). Snyder was fourth fastest, with 123.506 miles per hour, while Joe was in comfortably at 120.240. DeVore sneaked in with the thirty-third "fastest time."

As expected, Snyder and Householder disposed of the opposition early in the race and moved into a commanding lead. Then Snyder retired at 375 miles, and Householder lasted only four laps longer. Both cars went out with identical failures: the hoses connecting the blowers with the intake manifolds broke in the same place. Their boss cruised to ninth place. During the race Joe reported the goings-on to Sparks in the pits via ham radio channel W9XSA, which he had installed in the cockpit of his Offy.

With the race over, the pair of Sparks sixes was returned to Los Angeles for modifications. In July 1938 the organization moved into a bigger plant on San Fernando Road, and work was begun on a third car. The monstrous 1937 machine was given a new block and crank to reduce it from 337 to 271 cubic inches. The blower was scrapped, and Adams converted the two-man body into a single-seater.

This Big Six was for Joe. Snyder was reassigned to one of the blown cars, while the California star Rex Mays took Householder's place. Mel Hansen was given Thorne's old car, now equipped with a 270 Offy.

Though Householder was eager to compete at Indianapolis, he could not abide the arrogance and mercurial mood swings of his boss. He understood the potential of the Thorne cars, but could not negotiate a reasonable contract and, already having a solid income from driving midgets three or four times a week, left the team. He was to return in 1939 in a second-rate car and crashed during practice before failing to qualify. One final appearance at Indianapolis in 1948 was a disaster, and he left competition to become the head of Chrysler Corporation's motor sports program in the 1960s and 1970s.

By early 1939 the Thorne operation was at full boost as it prepared the two Sparks creations (called the "Little Sixes" by the press in contrast to the original 1937 Sparks Big Six that Joe planned to drive). After another year of development in the hands of Art Sparks, his crew had elevated the Snyder/Mays Little Sixes to the status of "favorite" prior to qualifications.

Between the two rivals, however, the Boyle operation did better in the actual race, with Chet Miller bringing his Offy-powered car home third, a result of consistent driving rather than outright speed. Bill Cummings, the leader of the team, lasted only 72 laps before a radiator leak sidelined him. Mauri Rose, driving the six-cylinder, underpowered 6CM Maserati that Cotton Henning had somehow purchased from the brothers, ran mid-pack for 165 laps before the engine's supercharger failed under the strain of running flat-out at over 120 miles an hour.

After disposing of the two Thorne cars and chief rivals Louie Meyer and Rex Mays, Van Nuys, California, veteran Floyd Roberts, who had started in the pole position, took command and went on to victory in the 1938 race. Driving alone for the five hundred miles without the mid-race relief driver often employed over the grueling distance, Roberts set a record-breaking average speed of 117.2 miles per hour and took home a whopping thirty-eight thousand dollars in prize money—an astounding amount in 1938 dollars, and more money than the entire New York Yankees baseball team would receive for winning the World Series later that year.

Wilbur Shaw, still at the wheel of his aged but reliable "pay car," was riding steadily in third place with only two laps left in the race. He followed Chet Miller, who held a seemingly insurmountable lead in second behind Roberts. But a last-minute pit stop dropped Boyle's Miller to third and raised the hometown Shaw to second place at the finish.

During the final months of 1938, the major Indianapolis teams regrouped for what was to be an increasingly competitive 1939 Indianapolis 500. The nation was slowly rising out of the Depression, with more disposable income available for such sports as big league motor racing. Moreover, the steady increase in defense spending by the Roosevelt administration—sensing the ever-growing threat of Nazi Germany—had energized the aircraft industry, with spin-off technology in metal alloys, fuel systems, rubber compounds, fuels, lubricants, and other arcane components that could be adapted from fighter planes to race cars.

While Mike Boyle and his team pursued success through the Maserati connection and Joe Thorne was throwing bags of money into his elaborate Los Angeles shop, other men were also arming themselves for the upcoming war of the wheels. Louie Meyer was working with California engine genius Bud Winfield after obtaining major funding from Indianapolis-based Bowes Seal Fast to create their Winfield-8 Special, which would prove to be as fast as any car ever to pound the speedway bricks. Crafty Floyd Roberts was planning to defend his 500 title with the same curly Wetteroth-built, Offy-powered machine that remained one of the rare dirt track machines capable of running with the Thorne and Winfield machines specifically designed for the sweeping corners at Indianapolis Motor Speedway.

But the Meyer and Roberts teams were struggling. Their Depression-stretched California operations were able to field only one contending automobile, while the Thorne team appeared in Gasoline Alley with two first-class automobiles backed by legions of technicians and engineers. Moreover, the nation's greatest race car designer and builder, Harry Miller, had returned for one last fling. On the edge of bankruptcy, he had engaged the Gulf Oil Company to fund the construction of two revolutionary four-wheel-drive, rear-engine machines powered by supercharged, straight-six engines reputed to produce more than 245 horsepower on regular 80-octane Gulf No-Nox pump gasoline. But unable to find a top driver, Miller had been forced to engage George Bailey, whose best finish in the 500 since 1934 had been a distant twelfth.

Even though Wilbur Shaw was committed to the Boyle Maserati, he coppered his bets by entering his own now-aged "pay car" for Mauri Rose. While the warhorse was now three years old and had been converted to a single-seater, it had won the race in 1937 and finished second in 1938, proving beyond all doubt to still be a contender.

Also on the entry list was the brilliant midget driver Bob Swanson at the wheel of the exquisite new Myron Stevens–fabricated Samson Special. In its engine bay was the powerful, supercharged V16 that the late, great Frank Lockhart had designed for his Stutz Blackhawk land speed record car. While on its way to seizing the record on April 25, 1928, at Daytona Beach, Florida, the car had blown a tire and crashed at over 250 miles an hour, killing Lockhart. The engine had been preserved and, eleven years later, was at Indianapolis in the Samson Special.

Also quietly in play was Shaw's new teammate, Ted Horn. Driving the same old, rebodied, front-driver Miller that had been in Boyle's stable for years, Eylard Theodore Horn had been born into a wealthy Cincinnati family twenty-nine years earlier and, after rejecting a bright career as a classical musician like his father, had gone to California to establish himself as a brilliant race driver on the dangerous Ascot oval in the Los Angeles suburbs. Having driven another ancient Miller to fourth place in 1938, Henning had engaged Horn for the team while attending the victory banquet after the race. A quiet, well-mannered gentleman, Horn was a fierce competitor, and though Shaw was pleased to have him on the team, he kept him at a distance, understanding that Horn possessed the will and the talent to win the big race if his own Maserati failed to live up to expectations.

Like most of the race drivers of the day, Ted Horn was wildly superstitious. Among the clan, green cars were taboo, as were black cats and the number thirteen. But beyond that, Horn refused to have his picture taken before a race and ardently kept children and women away from his car on the day of the event. (Women, for the most part, were banned from the pits in all American contests of the day, save for amateur sports car races, which were considered to be beneath contempt by the professional contingent.) But Horn's superstitions also included refusing to shave on race day and carrying a lucky dime in his right boot. Shoes were a common amulet; some drivers tied baby shoes to their cars' steering columns, and Wilbur Shaw refused to race without the aged, grease-and-rubber-stained brogues that he had worn in many victories.

Ted Horn's decision not to shave on race day had come with the 1936 death of his friend "Doc" MacKenzie at Milwaukee's one-mile dirt track. MacKenzie had raced for years with a smartly manicured goatee, but at the insistence of his new wife, he had razored away his facial hair the morning of the race, only to die hours later. This tragedy had convinced Horn—an otherwise highly intelligent and astute thinker—that shaving before facing the challenges of competition was a mark of bad luck.

It was into this mechanical battleground that Shaw entered in May 1939. He was at the wheel of a new automobile that on paper and according to the press carried imposing credentials. But for all its glamorous reputation, it had yet to prove itself in the fastest, most dangerous big-time automobile race on the planet. There being no safety components for the drivers beyond a simple leather helmet, men like Horn and Shaw drove racing cars in street clothes. Such devices as roll bars, fuel cells, shoulder harnesses, fireproof clothing, full-face helmets, crash-worth chassis, physical examinations, and other safety measures were unheard of. Men climbed into the cockpits understanding the inherent danger and willing to take such risks. They were classic examples of a human trait that essayist Alexis Carrell called "audacity" in the face of death. It was this component, claimed Carrell, that energized men to explore, to invade, to invent, to risk life and limb in the name of advancing civilization. Perhaps Carrell would not have included motor racing among his noble causes, but in terms of risk-taking based on his unique human trait of audacity, the sport/business engaged in by Shaw and others would surely have qualified.

7

THE WAR BEGINS

SPRINGTIME IN INDIANA can be magic. The temperatures linger in the mid-seventies, and the humidity that suffocates the open plains of the Midwest lies a few months ahead. Aside from the occasional thunderstorm that rumbles out of the Mississippi basin, day after day of bright sunshine lit up the Indianapolis Motor Speedway when the track opened for practice on the first week in 1939.

The rows of wooden garages in Gasoline Alley that had been constructed twenty years earlier were already filled with race cars and loads of spare parts brought along by the individual teams. Workbenches were layered with veritable buffets of shining tools as well as the omnipresent hot plates and coffeepots that would offer a constant source of energy as the mechanics prepared themselves for work around the clock. In some cases sleeping bags and cots had been spread beside the race cars in preparation for the endless hours of labor.

To the newcomer the garages appeared to be stalls of the type found at major horse tracks and thoroughbred farms. Like so much of American motor sports, the link to horse racing was vivid and ongoing. Most tracks in the nation had originally been built for horses, and many fairgrounds' ovals were still multipurpose. Racing for both horses and automobiles involved running dirt-surfaced tracks ranging from a quarter mile to one mile in length. The Indianapolis Motor Speedway was the great exception—2.5 miles in length and originally surfaced with bricks, although only the thirty-three-hundred-foot front straightaway still remained unpaved with smoother macadam. Contrary to all European races for both horses and cars, the Brickyard retained the unique American tradition of running counterclockwise on oval-like, closed circuits. In Europe automobiles ran clockwise, with a few exceptions, on long, open courses over hill and dale, retaining a closer relationship with nature and real-world transportation.

Although American auto racing took place mainly on aged dirt horse tracks, the Indianapolis Motor Speedway had been purposely built in 1909 for both racing and testing for the nascent local automobile industry. At that time the city was competing with Detroit to become the center of the car business, and in fact more than sixty manufacturers had started there—only to fail—including the famed Duesenberg, Marmon, and Stutz brands.

Across Sixteenth Street from the speedway was a row of diners and saloons, where off-hours would be spent sharing tales and adventures accumulated on the dusty racing trail that spread from coast to coast. Farther east on the broad thoroughfare lay downtown Indianapolis and the elegant Claypool and Antlers Hotels, where the likes of Mike Boyle, Joe Thorne, and other wealthy car owners and sponsors spent their evenings. Many of the drivers rented rooms in private homes, while others bunked in with friends, it being a Depression-based economy, where little extra money was available for anything but basic accommodations.

Many of the drivers lived in Southern California, where racing went on at various dirt tracks throughout the year, permitting them to hone their talents without seasonal interruptions. Even many of those who claimed residence in the Midwest spent their winters in the Golden State, either racing or working in the Los Angeles shops where engines, race cars, and special components were manufactured. Unless a driver was able to gain a "ride" with a major team or somehow win a major race like the Indianapolis 500, trying to survive simply on the winnings gained in competition bordered on the impossible. An exclusive few, like Joel Thorne, came from family money. But for the most part, racing drivers of the day had middle-class backgrounds with minimal financial backing.

It was a vagabond life, moving from track to track in search of success. Rooming houses, tourist homes, cheap hotels, and friends' back bedrooms were the essentials of life, coupled with food and drink in roadside cafes and cheap diners. With the entire nation mired in the Depression and the number of unemployed in the millions, men who could somehow eke out a living by driving a race car, regardless of the incessant threat of injury, viewed themselves as among the fortunate—choosing to ignore the reality that statistically one-third of those who engaged in the sport/business of professional automobile racing faced a violent death, with no possible chance of insurance benefits for their survivors.

A few of these drivers resided in Indianapolis, having made enough money in racing and associated trades to purchase homes. Hoosier native Shaw, with his second wife, Mary, called "Boots" by her family and friends, had bought a cute bungalow in the suburb of Speedway a few blocks from the track, thanks to his winnings from the recent 500. As a struggling young driver, Shaw had spent much of his time in California, racing at Ascot and other tracks in Los Angeles, where the sport was extremely popular. Moreover, many of the best race car fabricators, engine builders, and designers worked in the area, making it a perfect base of operations for young men who were seeking to advance in the trade. But now Shaw had moved back to his native state and, except for the Indianapolis 500, had essentially ceased racing. Having made a small fortune with his Indianapolis victory, and having been hired to promote such consumer products as Champion spark plugs and Perfect Circle piston rings, Shaw and Boots were able to live comfortably without his risking life and limb on the rough-and-tumble "bull ring" dirt tracks of the nation. While remaining fit via a regular physical fitness regimen, Shaw restricted his race driving to the month of May at his hometown track, where, through skill and experience, he knew that with the right machine he could match anybody in terms of speed and endurance.

With the Maserati stabled in one of the three garages in Gasoline Alley assigned to Mike Boyle, Cotton Henning began his meticulous preparation for the 1939 qualifying runs—a four-lap, ten-mile ride around the giant track against the clock. Thirty-three of the fastest would make the race, while the remaining sixteen in the entry field of forty-nine would be sent home in shame. Based on the unofficial practice times recorded by Shaw, it appeared that his Maserati had more than enough power to make the starting field. But uncertainty lingered, based on the possibility of mechanical failure—or worse yet, a crash. After all, the car had already suffered damage at the hands of Freddie Zehender in Italy, and even an expert like Shaw lived with the possibility of losing control on the high-speed Indianapolis corners, as he had done in 1932 or, more recently, at the Vanderbilt Cup two years earlier. Driving an automobile with skinny, ironlike compound tires on greasy pavement surfaces at the very edge of control—the "ragged edge," as many called it—offered an incessant opportunity for error and a major accident.

No such incidents happened until the eighth day of practice. Car builder and designer Harry Miller, the acknowledged genius of American racing, was in deep decline because of failing health and the agonies of the Depression, which had reduced his once-proud firm to a tiny cadre of loyalist helpers. His last fling had begun in 1938, thanks to the infusion of funds from the Gulf Oil Company, which backed him in the design and construction of three radical machines intended to contest at Indianapolis and on the European Grand Prix circuit.

The trio of Millers that appeared at Indianapolis Motor Speedway in 1939 represented breakthrough engineering, with four-wheel-drive and supercharged six-cylinder engines mounted behind the driver as in the German Auto Unions. But the Gulf Oil officials had demanded that the engines run not on the potent methanol racing fuel commonly used in racing engines but on their No-Nox 80-octane pump gasoline employed in passenger cars. This limited horsepower to 245, while the Sparks/Thorne cars of Snyder and Mays produced over 400 horsepower. Moreover, for reasons that made no sense, Miller believed that a low center of gravity on race cars limited handling. He absurdly maintained that a tall car would generate "side-bite" on the outside rear wheels and increase cornering power. Therefore the Gulf Millers were gawky, high-sided machines with the driver sitting high in the airstream over the driveshaft.

One of the assigned drivers, Zeke Meyer, immediately quit the team, claiming his car was uncontrollable. Then teammate Johnny Seymour hit the wall in turn three, causing one of the fuel tanks dangerously mounted on the side of the chassis to explode. The car was consumed in flames, but Seymour managed to escape with only minor burns. He walked away from the sport, never to drive again.

Somehow George Bailey, in the third Gulf Miller, deciphered the weird handling and managed to qualify sixth at 125 miles per hour. He would join two of Mike Boyle's teammates—Ted Horn and Chet Miller—in the second row of starters for the five-hundred-mile race.

Wilbur Shaw remained the leader for Boyle in the Maserati, but he privately entered his own veteran "pay car" that had carried him to victory in 1937 and to second place a year later. He assigned old friend Mauri Rose to the car, understanding that the little Detroiter was capable of winning, even with an outdated machine. Rose had in fact finished second in 1932 and fourth in 1936 and was known as one of the bravest and most aggressive drivers in the business. He would later go on to win the 500 twice and become a respected engineer for General Motors after his retirement from competition.

Although the local press nattered incessantly about the Maserati—which, they noted, was the first "foreign" automobile to threaten the American-built machinery since the early 1920s—it was obvious to Shaw that he had serious, if not overwhelming, competition. Louie Meyer, though a long-time friend, was hardly ready to step aside as a contender. He was, after all, the only man to win the 500 three times and had been a serious player in every race since his first victory in 1928. In 1938 he had run with the leaders until the oil pump on his powerful new Winfield-8 with a supercharged engine collapsed on the 149th lap. He was back with the same car and would give no quarter to the European invader. So, too, for Thorne team leader Jimmy Snyder and his Art

Sparks–designed, supercharged, six-cylinder machine and his backup, the brilliant charger from California and crowd favorite Rex Mays in the sister machine.

Meyer threw down the gauntlet first in qualifying. Up to that year the entrants had been required to run against the clock for ten laps or twenty-five miles. But as the Depression had hammered at the budgets of the racers, the speedway management cut the laps to four with the intent to save fuel and tires. Running the big Winfield with wild abandon, Meyer shattered the track record and became the first man to break the 130-mile-per-hour barrier—a speed that seemed impossible even five years earlier.

Then Jimmy Snyder rolled onto the track carrying a reputation as a hot qualifier, a man who could drive at the limit around the most dangerous stretch of pavement in the world. When he finished his four laps, stopwatches clicked along pit row to confirm that he had taken the fast time away from Meyer by less than a second at 130.167 miles per hour. Teammate Rex Mays tried to do the same in the Thorne sister car but aborted his run with spark plug trouble; nevertheless, he was still considered a contender when the actual race started.

Joe Thorne took the wheel of the original Sparks Big Six, and although the machine had more than enough power under its hood, its extra weight (having been converted from a two-man car), coupled with Joe's limited driving skills, doomed it to start in twentieth position and reach a top speed of only 122 miles per hour, or eight miles an hour off teammate Snyder's record speed.

Shaw and Henning counted three rivals—Meyer, Snyder, and Mays—as their real opposition when the Maserati took the green flag for its four-lap qualifying run. Driving carefully in a car that still remained unfamiliar, Shaw set the third fastest time, at 128.977 miles per hour, which was slower than Snyder and Meyer, but he was supremely confident that he could run with the leaders during the race.

On Memorial Day of 1939 the city of Indianapolis became the center of the Heartland. More than one hundred thousand men and women from all over the Midwest poured into the city, jamming hotels and tourist homes while camping out in parks and on the lawns of private homes across the city and the adjacent suburb of Speedway, where the giant track was located. The relaxed joy of the Memorial Day holiday blanked out the alarming news from overseas that both the Germans and the Japanese were on a full-scale war footing.

In America the labor unrest in Detroit and elsewhere had stimulated expansion of the Communist Party in the salons of New York and among the Hollywood elite. The crazed Fascist Fritz Kuhn had organized the American Bund movement in support of Adolf Hitler, and in February twenty-two thousand of his supporters had filled New York's Madison Square Garden for a rally draped with Nazi swastikas. A month later Hitler's Wehrmacht seized Czechoslovakia. As the teams drifted into the speedway at Indianapolis for a month of high-speed sport, Hitler and Italy's pompous dictator, Benito Mussolini, were signing a military treaty they pronounced the "Pact of Steel." Meanwhile,

Hitler's high command was finalizing plans for an invasion of Poland in the coming September that would trigger World War II, at least in Europe and the Far East, while America remained arrogantly and naively out of the fray.

While throngs gathered at the Indianapolis Motor Speedway for the twenty-seventh running of the 500, multitudes were on Long Island's Flushing Meadows, where the New York World's Fair had opened on April 30. Already more than one million spectators had entered the gates of the extravaganza that showcased an art deco paradise of the future. In Manhattan engineers at the National Broadcasting Company (NBC) were making final preparations to broadcast to a small gathering of executives and journalists a prototype visual-imaging process that would be known as "television," a technology that had been discussed and written about in scientific circles for more than a decade.*

On the thirteenth of the month the Hamburg-Amerika (sic) steamship SS *St. Louis* had left Hamburg with 937 Jewish citizens whom the Nazi party had permitted to emigrate to Cuba. But the Caribbean island government had refused their entry, and the ship had been forced to European ports, where most of the passengers were ultimately murdered in the Nazi extermination camps. The tragic journey would be recounted in the 1962 best-selling novel *Ship of Fools* by Katherine Anne Porter.

---

* The author's father, Raymond F. Yates, published the first major book on the subject (*ABC of Television*, New York: Norman Henley Publishing, 1929).

On May 2, New York Yankees slugger Lou Gehrig had given a teary good-bye to his fans after playing in 2,130 consecutive games. He had been diagnosed with a rare muscular disease that would ultimately take his life. Meanwhile, most Americans were still struggling against the grim reality of the Depression. Nearly 17 percent of adults remained unemployed, and only 3 percent made enough money to pay a federal income tax (in fact, 670,000 of the richest paid 90 percent of the tax). Fewer than 60 percent owned an automobile, and most of those vehicles were older than five years and on the edge of the junkyard.

On Memorial Day 1939, the vast parking lots spread over the infield of the Indianapolis Motor Speedway were clogged with rusty Model-T Fords, beat-up Chevrolets, Essexes, and Hudsons that had been patched together in order to transport the crowds to the single major annual sporting event that many of them were able to afford. As the marching bands thumped noisily along the brick-paved straightaway during the prerace ceremony, the teams huddled in Gasoline Alley making final preparations. It was a warm day, and Shaw, like most of the drivers, planned to run the race in a long-sleeved work shirt and light cotton pants, oblivious to the deadly tank of methanol-alcohol fuel mounted behind his seat. The rest of the drivers had adopted his use of a crash helmet, but most still refused to use a seat belt, believing that ejection from a crashing car was safer than remaining in the cockpit.

Henning filled the Maserati's sixty-gallon fuel tank while other crewmen hauled six ten-gallon milk cans to the pits along the track. They would be used to refill the car during the race, it having been calculated that at five miles to the gallon, the hungry Maserati would swill more than one hundred gallons of volatile liquid. At least three pit stops were planned, not only for refueling, but to change the four specially designed Firestone tires that had been mounted on all thirty-three cars.

The men were alone now, women being forbidden in both Gasoline Alley and along pit row. While in Europe females were allowed in such precincts, and even occasionally raced with the men, the separation of the sexes at Indianapolis was a rigid rule that would not be altered until the 1960s. In a day when feminism and multiculturalism are totally accepted in motor racing, as well as in all other aspects of advanced societies, it is difficult to accept the fact that places like the garage area at Indianapolis were at one time rigidly all-male precincts. Even then, nurses stationed at the small on-track hospital were banned from the place, making the Indianapolis Motor Speedway's inner sanctums as essentially all-white and all-male as the Ku Klux Klan, which by the way, had active Klaverns, or local chapters, across the Hoosier state during the 1930s.

Mike Boyle's car was ready for the race by the time he arrived in Gasoline Alley in the company of a hard-looking man who said nothing but was obviously packing a large automatic pistol under his suit coat. Henning and Shaw assured Boyle that the car was ready to contend for the lead, but their strategy was to let Meyer and Snyder battle in the early stages, perhaps to either break their cars or consume too much fuel or too many tires, while Shaw cruised steadily in their wakes.

Five hundred miles was hardly a sprint. Winning at Indianapolis required carefully conceived strategies, based on the potentials of both car and driver plus track conditions and, more important, the competition. Other men in the starting field had the ability to run with Shaw in heads-up competition, and it was up to Henning to control the pace via pit signals to Shaw while calculating stops for fuel and tires to prepare the big red machine for a flat-out charge for the lead during the final fifty miles of the contest.

Boyle was confident that his trio—Shaw, Henning, and the Maserati—composed the best possible team to win the race. He stepped into the sunny morning and left the garage to head for his reserved seat in the grandstands knowing that the funds he had bilked and stolen outright from his union's victims would be well spent at the world's most prestigious automobile race. Based on today's dollars, victory at Indianapolis would pay back Mike Boyle well over a million dollars once the prize money was added to the endorsement from Firestone and other sponsors, plus appearance fees, auto shows, and other financial benefits that would last well into the following year. The Indianapolis 500 was not only the biggest single-day sporting event in the world, but it was also the most lucrative for the winner. Even after half the prize money would be shared by Shaw, Henning, and members of the crew, Boyle was sure to pocket enough money to reimburse himself for the Maserati purchase, with a fancy profit for the entire enterprise—provided victory came as planned.

But the gamble was severe. If the car crashed, blew its engine, or simply did not live up to performance expectations and finished deep in the pack, Boyle could lose tens of thousands of his ill-gotten gains.

Most of the race car owners at Indianapolis had little interest in financial gain. The gamble of parlaying an entry in an automobile race into a big reward made even less sense than entering a thoroughbred horse in the Kentucky Derby. At least for the horse owner, breeding stock might recoup some of the massive investment in operating the vast farms that were necessary to develop competitive mares and stallions. Not so with racing cars. With no capacity for breeding, each machine had to be hand built with painstaking care, backed by stunning amounts of capital.

Most of Boyle's rivals were rich boys like Joe Thorne and Gil Pirrung (the heir to a Pittsburgh steel fortune), both of whom spent millions over the decade to have automobiles designed and constructed by expert craftsmen. Others, like Boyle, simply purchased existing machines, either from other car owners or from small factories like that owned by the Maserati brothers. There were perhaps thirty such men in America who had the money and enthusiasm to buy or have built racing cars for the Indianapolis 500. The odds of them ever enjoying a profit from such a venture rose to the impossible, but this meant nothing, based on their love of the sport and the chance to compete with the best in the world.

This surely was Mike Boyle's reason for playing the racing game. His competitive spirit far transcended any thought of profit. A hard-edged businessman within his union and the political and underworld wars in Chicago, Boyle engaged in motor sport strictly as a diversion that was totally disconnected from his daily reality, where amusement and sportsmanship were nonexistent. Unlike the wealthy men who participated in horse racing and backed up their efforts with massive stud farms, there was no chance for Boyle to profit from his automobiles unless he chose to build and sell extras, which made no financial sense, or to sell his successful machines for profit, which again bordered on the impossible. The horsemen who competed at Churchill Downs, Saratoga, and other venues sometimes made money on the sale of their racehorses, but for the most part they engaged in the sport for pleasure, as did men like Mike Boyle at Indianapolis.

8

VICTORY AT THE BRICKYARD

EACH OF THE thirty-three men who faced the challenge of the Indianapolis 500 on Memorial Day 1939 did so in their own unique way. There being no safety rules other than the requirements of wearing a crash helmet (still not used in Europe), the drivers entered the grueling contest as if they were driving to work. On that warm spring day, Wilbur Shaw climbed into the cockpit of the Boyle Maserati wearing a long-sleeved work shirt, khaki slacks, and the grease-stained shoes he had worn for good luck for the past seven years. Although some drivers drove barehanded, Shaw carefully coated his hands with talcum powder before donning his leather gloves, hoping to prevent the blisters and bloody palms that could result from rough sawing on the large, wood-rimmed steering wheel.

Weighing less than 120 pounds, Shaw worked feverishly to overcome his disadvantage in the size and strength demanded in controlling an unruly beast that when full of fuel, oil, and water weighed well over a ton. He had developed his own fitness machine—a steering wheel mounted to a shock absorber that when twisted for hours of exercise, developed the upper body strength needed for muscling the brutish machine in a day when power steering was unheard of in the world of automobiles.

He and Henning arrived at their garage in Gasoline Alley early on race morning to make a final check of the Maserati and to examine the stack of spare Firestone tires that would be used during the race. The small cadre of crewmen wandered in later, to be joined by Mike Boyle and his bodyguard an hour before the start of the race at eleven o'clock local time.

As the maroon Maserati was rolled into the fresh Indiana sunlight, Shaw chattered casually with his friend Louie Meyer, whose sleek white, red, and black Bowes Seal Fast Special was housed in an adjacent garage. Shaw understood that if anyone were to beat him to the checkered flag, it would be either Meyer, who already had three victories in the 500 under his belt, or Jimmy Snyder, in the immensely powerful new Sparks–Thorne Engineering Special poking its shiny blue nose out of its stall a few feet away.

But Snyder, while fast, hardly scared Louie Meyer, whose confidence rose to uncanny heights. Born of German immigrants in New York in 1904, he had been raised in Los

Angeles, where his machinist father had moved the family when he was four years old. His skills with tools were immediately apparent, and by the time he was twenty, his reputation as an auto mechanic was widely known, especially among the racers who competed at the Legion Ascot Speedway, located in the Alhambra suburb. But by the early 1920s he had traded his tools for a seat in various racing cars, quickly establishing himself as a skillful and relentless competitor.

It was during this period that Meyer developed a strong friendship with Shaw, a rival on the tracks but a compatriot among the California racing community. In 1926 Meyer accompanied Shaw to Indianapolis, where he served as mechanic on Shaw's Jynx Special, a veteran dirt track machine that would hardly be a contender for victory. In fact, during the middle of the race an exhausted Shaw gave up his seat to Meyer, who then drove the Jynx for forty-one laps in a day when no particular qualifications were necessary to compete. Displaying skills as a driver, two years later, in 1927, Louie Meyer won the AAA National Championship, and a year later he took first place in the 500, thereby establishing himself as a major star on a meteoric rise to fame.

Serving as both driver and chief mechanic on his cars, Meyer's unique combination of talents gave him an advantage over many of his competitors, including Shaw, who contested him for the lead in the 1933 Indy 500, with Meyer winning his second victory while Shaw chased him home in second place. His unprecedented third win at Indianapolis came three years later. Meyer's victories stemmed in part from the power and reliability of engineering genius Harry Miller's simple, reliable four- and eight-cylinder engines mounted in conventional chassis of the day. But by 1937 it was obvious to Meyer that such engine-chassis combinations were becoming obsolete. He was aware of Mike Boyle's contacts with the Maserati brothers in Italy and Joe Thorne's massive effort in California. If he wanted a fourth win at Indianapolis before retiring, Louie Meyer, now thirty-three and beginning to feel his age against the young lions who were absorbing the brutal beating of riding a cart-sprung machine over the speedway's lumpy bricks for five hundred miles, would have to employ his mechanical skills to create a racing car to compete with his rivals.

Working with Fred Offenhauser, who had been Harry Miller's chief engineer until taking over his sagging business in the Depression-dulled year of 1933; his brilliant draftsman, Leo Goosen; and engine specialist Bud Winfield and his carburetor-specialist brother, Ed, Meyer devised a straight-eight, 183-cubic-inch, supercharged engine based on the previous designs of Miller and Offenhauser. But although the supercharged engine had enormous power, in the five-hundred-horsepower range, its conventional, leaf-sprung suspension was a bear to handle in the corner, and even under Meyer's skillful hands, he was able to qualify only in twelfth place for the 1938 Indianapolis 500. An oil pump then failed at 149 laps in the actual race, dropping Meyer to a twelfth-place finish. However, thanks to the generous sponsorship of local industrialist Robert Bowes, who owned Bowes Seal Fast, Meyer was amply financed for another assault on the speedway in 1939, still eager to become the first man to win the famed race four times.

Meyer was a head taller than Shaw and had large, calloused mechanic's hands and a well-muscled upper body that would play to his advantage in the long, grueling race. Though he and Shaw carefully chose not to share strategies, both understood that Snyder would probably play the "rabbit" in the early stages, setting a pace of nearly 130 miles an hour in hopes of forcing Shaw and Meyer, as well as Ted Horn, hotshot Rex Mays, and other contenders, into a car-breaking chase.

Shaw understood the risks in such a strategy, in that it would consume both tires and fuel at dangerous levels, perhaps forcing an extra pit stop late in the race. Therefore, he and Henning devised a more conservative plan. Understanding that the Maserati was still essentially undeveloped for the speedway and in the hands of a driver who was not yet fully comfortable with the new machine— which the local press endlessly referred to as the first "foreign" car to contend in the 500 for more than twenty years—they would set a pace of 126 miles per hour, or about three miles an hour slower than Shaw's qualifying speed. At that pace the Maserati would burn about a gallon of its methanol-alcohol fuel every five miles. With it's tank carrying sixty gallons, a range of three hundred miles was theoretically possible, but hauling around a full tank would demand extra tire wear, which in turn might mean an extra stop for fresh rubber. Henning and Shaw decided to set up the Maserati to carry between thirty-five and forty gallons, keeping the car lighter between the three required pit stops that would have to be made in order to mount fresh tires. Such a plan would be unable to deal with such hazards as an engine failure or a broken suspension piece caused by the constant hammering on the rough brick surface of the main straightaway, the rest of the speedway having been paved with macadam two years earlier to reduce the incessant pounding on both the automobiles and ever-suffering drivers.

An hour before the start of the 1939 race, Henning and the crew pushed the Maserati out of Gasoline Alley and onto the vast front straightaway in the shadow of the immense grandstands, now clogged with more than one hundred thousand fans, who had come from all over the nation to see what somebody coined as "The Greatest Spectacle in Racing." Another fifty thousand spectators were scattered around the vast infield, having driven their cars through the gates at sunrise to find prime viewing locations around the fence lining the inside of the track.

The Indiana University marching band was thumping through a medley of John Phillip Sousa classics as the thirty-three multicolored machines were shoved silently into their starting positions, three by three, along the brick surface. With his three cars starting second, third, and fourth in the hands of Shaw, Ted Horn, and Chet Miller, Mike Boyle was in a jolly mood, his customary bowler traded for a straw boater and his vest unbuttoned. Chicago and the rugged life in the street seemed far away. News had come that his occasional enemy and sometime partner in the "business," Big Al Capone, had been released from Alcatraz after eleven years behind bars. He had been indicted for income tax evasion of $231,000 in 1930, a victim of a new and effective government strategy for nailing big-time gangsters, not for crime but for failing to report and pay levies on their ill-gotten gains. Ravaged by syphilis no doubt passed on by a prostitute in the Roaring Twenties, Capone would spend eight more years at his Miami estate, his mind pulverized by the disease, before dying in 1947.

While he understood that the Internal Revenue Service, the FBI, and other agencies were hovering over him and his union, Boyle was able to separate his shady business dealings in the Windy City from his love of motor racing. Surely he was using the expenses involved in campaigning his cars in the Indianapolis 500 and other major races to conceal income. The feds no doubt understood this dodge, but try as they might, after endless tax audits and periodic arrests for minor charges, Mike Boyle remained a free man. By then he had long since discarded the umbrella he had used in the early days as a repository for bribes, but it refused to die as the source of his nickname.

A back ailment had caused him to occasionally employ a cane while at Indianapolis.

In the tight little world of Indianapolis motor sport, Mike Boyle was safe. Neither his friends nor his rivals in racing—not even the press that covered the event—cared much about his dark reputation in Chicago. To them he was simply another gregarious, free-spending race car owner who financed the sport. Without rich men like him, there would be no Indianapolis 500. The source of their incomes—be it family money like Joe Thorne's or the Bowes family, whose Bowes Seal Fast backed Louie Meyer's efforts, or that of Umbrella Mike, known simply as a "union leader"—meant nothing to the racing establishment. Mike Boyle was another high roller who kept the sport afloat thanks to his deep pockets. Nothing more. Nothing less. Newsmen covering the race found Boyle to be openly accessible for interviews, as long as the subject centered on racing and never drifted into his Chicago "business" interests. They always referred to him as Umbrella Mike, and with his Irish gift of gab, Mike Boyle was a dependable source for quotes and comments about the upcoming race. Both he and Wilbur Shaw were open, articulate conversationalists, ever ready to be interviewed by the press for printable quotes.

As each of the drivers was introduced over the loudspeaker system, a wild cheer rose from the grandstands, especially for former winners Meyer and Shaw. Both men waved back as they slid into their leather seats and donned their crash helmets. Before the race the two rivals had made a bet in Gasoline Alley—one hundred dollars going to the one who led the first lap of the race, providing of course one of them could hold off the other starter in the front row. Jimmy Snyder had a wide reputation as a "charger." Among those who bet on which man would lead the opening lap, the big money was laid not on Meyer or Shaw, but on Snyder and his powerful Thorne Engineering Special.

After introducing the last of the drivers, Billy DeVore, who would start in the final position of thirty-third, track owner Captain Eddie Rickenbacker stepped to the microphone and uttered the traditional cry for action: "Gentlemen, start your engines!" Henning had already struck the hand crank into the snout of the Maserati. Unlike a number of the other cars that used the newly developed portable electric starters, the Maserati brothers retained the traditional crank that had been a component of the automobile since the first models had hit the roads a half a century earlier. With the big eight-cylinder engine already primed and in perfect tune, it took Henning less than half a turn of the crank before the monster came to life, its chrome-plated exhaust pipe blatting imperiously to join the cacophony of the other supercharged eights and guttural fours that now echoed through the stands.

Henning and Boyle moved to the cockpit to give Shaw rough pats on his shoulder for good luck and then moved back to Horn and Miller to offer similar but cursory good tidings. Rickenbacker then drove the Studebaker pace car onto the speedway as the front-row cars of Snyder,

Meyer, and Shaw rolled away. Two slow pace laps would unfold to form up the field and to permit the massive crowd to get a close-up look at the cars and drivers before they become a multihued blur at 150 miles an hour.

At the end of the second pace lap, Rickenbacker eased the Studebaker onto pit row and the rumble of the race cars deepened as throttles opened. Ahead of them on the edge of the track, midway on the front straight, starter Seth Klein held up a large green flag. As the field growled toward him, gaining speed, he whipped the flag downward and the race was on. As expected, Jimmy Snyder, on board the quickest car and holding the inside line into the first corner, grabbed the lead. The owner of a popular saloon on Chicago's west side, he had brought with him thousands of fans, who whooped and hollered above the din as he led the first lap by three car lengths over Meyer, with Shaw trailing in third. Surging through the field was Rex Mays, who had started mid-pack but had now found the missing power in the second Sparks-Thorne six and was gobbling up the distance between himself and the leaders. After a scramble for position within the first few laps, the field settled down with only Mays slicing forward. Snyder led, with Meyer close behind and Shaw riding steadily in third. The two other Boyle cars, driven by Miller and Horn, were nicely placed in the top five, while Mauri Rose, in Shaw's old machine, held a steady eighth.

Forty laps into the race Snyder stopped for fuel and tires as the remainder of the field drifted in and out of the pits for similar maintenance. This placed Meyer in the lead, while Shaw kept the Maserati under rein and reeled off consistent laps in keeping with his plan to maintain a steady pace. After stops by Meyer and Shaw, Jimmy Snyder regained the lead until pitting again on the 103rd lap, or just halfway beyond the 250-mile mark. This returned Meyer to first place, while Shaw eased into second. Snyder remained in the pits for an extended stop as Art Sparks frantically changed the six fouled spark plugs in the engine.

Four laps later, on the 107th, disaster struck. Up to that point the race had been unusually safe, with only a few harmless spins and no shredded metal or injuries. But then young Bob Swanson, an upcoming midget driver, who had taken the wheel of veteran Ralph Hepburn's Offy-powered Hamilton-Harris Special as a relief driver (not uncommon when drivers suffered from fatigue or from heat, exhaust fumes, and the general pounding of the body), lost control as he entered the backstretch. After fighting for command over his car, Swanson helplessly rode it into the inner fence, where a rear-end impact ignited the fuel tank and sent the flaming car tumbling onto the track and tossing the driver onto the pavement.

Riding on the tail of Swanson's car was defending 500 champion Floyd Roberts, in the same Curly Wetteroth–built Offy that he had driven to victory the year before. But this May the car had experienced a mass of mechanical ailments, and Roberts had qualified deep in the field in twenty-third position. Now scrambling mid-pack, he clipped the tail of Swanson's spinning machine, and his car pitched over the outside wall. Landing upside down, the impact broke Roberts's neck, instantly killing him.

The death of an Indianapolis 500 winner was far from unusual. Since the race had begun in 1911, seven of the twenty-three winners had died at the wheel on racetracks, and an eighth, Wild Bill Cummings, had lost his life in a highway accident. But among those fatalities, none had taken place at the great Indianapolis Motor Speedway, but rather on other tracks around the nation. And one—brilliant, young Frank Lockhart—had occurred on the ocean beach at Daytona, Florida, while seeking the land speed record on April 15, 1928.

The shocking death of Floyd Roberts, the defending champion of the 500, on the site of his greatest triumph the year earlier, stunned the nation, once more bringing the country's anti-auto-racing press to full cry, demanding that the sport be outlawed. Despite their cries and support in the halls of Congress, the sport enjoyed the backing of the major auto industry in Detroit. Other commercial enterprises also valued racing as a sales tool. Therefore, anti-racing legislation never gained serious political support.

Arriving on the scene within a fraction of a second, Chet Miller spun to avoid Swanson, who was lying directly in his path. Yanking the steering wheel hard to the left, Miller sent his Boyle Special plunging into the infield, where it crashed hard, seriously injuring him. With one driver dead and two others hurt, the yellow flag was signaled, forcing the remaining competitors to reduce speed and hold position while the debris was cleaned up.

The caution flag flew for over half an hour while the race unfolded at low speeds. With Meyer in front, Shaw directly behind him, and Snyder riding third (but a lap behind due to several unscheduled stops), the race was to be restarted in what would be a mad dash to the finish.

Mike Boyle fretted over what to do. He had known Chet Miller for years and considered him an integral part of his team. Having been told by the emergency crews that his driver was seriously hurt, with numerous broken bones, lacerations, and a possible fractured skull, Boyle briefly considered leaving the speedway to join Miller at the nearby Methodist Hospital. But on the track, with the drivers and their cars preparing to resume the race, Shaw, now in second place, was clearly in contention to win the race in a final sprint against Meyer. After conferring with Henning, Boyle decided there was little he could do for Miller, so he remained in the Shaw pits, where the glory of once again winning the greatest motor race in the world possibly awaited him.

At this point Shaw had familiarized himself with the Maserati, and Henning had made several adjustments to the tire pressures that had helped to maximize the car's handling. Because Henning had reduced supercharger pressure and cut maximum horsepower in the name of reliability, Meyer's big straight-eight Winfield had the advantage on the long straights. But in the speedway's four sweeping corners, Shaw's Maserati was able to run faster, forcing Meyer to drive on the ragged edge to hold his lead. Driving harder and harder to stay in front, Meyer began to wear down his tires, while the steady Shaw, a generally calm and polite man off the track, but a fierce and tenacious competitor, snubbed against the tail of the Bowes Special. With sixteen laps remaining, Shaw rode high on the outside groove of the track and swept past Meyer down the front stretch. Running side by side for a lap, Meyer had to give his rival and friend the lead. Then the three-time champion shredded his worn right rear tire and tore into his pit for a quick change. Now a lap behind, but with the bit still in his teeth and riding on fresh tires, Meyer unreeled a series of wild laps at over 130 miles per hour, sliding the big Bowes Special through the sweeping corners in a seemingly futile effort to run down Shaw.

With just two laps remaining, Meyer lost control of the Bowes as he exited the second turn at roughly the same place where Swanson had earlier triggered the Roberts crash. Looping wildly to the left, the brute slammed the low fence on the inside of the track, nose first, tipping the machine on its side and flinging Meyer out of the cockpit at over 120 miles per hour. He would later claim, "As I flew through the air, I thought, *Enough of this madness!* I guess I was the only driver ever to retire while I was in midair."

Miraculously, Meyer landed on the soft infield grass and as his car slid to a stop on its wheels, its engine dead. The great driver rose to his feet and waited for the emergency crew's ambulance. Once inside, he was judged to be uninjured other than scuffed knees and hands. As Meyer shook himself off, someone asked him, "Where are your shoes?"

"What do you mean?" asked Meyer before he looked down to discover that he was standing in his socks. It was later discovered, after his car had been towed back to Gasoline Alley, that Meyer had been pitched out of the cockpit with such force that he had literally been propelled out of his shoes. They remained in the cockpit, their laces still tied.

How a man could be tossed from an automobile traveling at better than twice a mile a minute and survive without injury defies the laws of physics. Add to that the kinetic forces that yanked him out of his shoes during the tumble, and the entire incident makes no sense. Yet a series of photos recorded the crash and confirmed that Meyer somehow exited the tumbling machine at exactly the right moment to land, balletlike, on the loamy grass without injury. Being a sensible man, Meyer no doubt believed that he had consumed all his reserves of good fortune during that bizarre exit, adding to his conviction to retire on the spot.

While hard to believe, Meyer's high-speed exit was not unusual. In a day when seat belts and other safety equipment beyond a helmet were unknown (and still not required in Europe, where cloth caps to prevent hair messing was the rule of the day), other men had been pitched from race cars with little or no injury. This only added to the conventional thinking that remaining in a crashing automobile was more dangerous than leaving, no matter how violent that exit might be. Seat belts were not to be commonly employed until the 1950s, and fireproof clothing did not arrive on the scene until the next decade. Today's race drivers are encapsulated in crash-resistant pods, wrapped up in advanced clothing and helmets, and surrounded by roll bars that protect them in the violent crashes. When it is considered that Indianapolis cars now negotiate the curve where Meyer's crash occurred at nearly 100 miles an hour faster, the possibility of being flung from a car without injury borders on the impossible.

That said, Louie Meyer's retirement from the sport that had made him a wealthy and famous man was among the most unique in the history of racing. However, his Winfield Special, despite its violent rollover, would be repaired under the hands of Rex Mays and would continue to be a contender at Indianapolis until the early 1950s. Such was the life span of racing cars of the day, built and designed when engineering was in a status to be unbroken another twenty years.

Louie Meyer never sat in a racing car again, but he hardly gave up his deep involvement in the sport that had gained him fame and fortune. After all, in thirteen years he had recorded 5,249 miles at high speed around the Indianapolis Motor Speedway, highlighted by three victories. He was employed by the Ford Motor Company to oversee the rebuilding of Ford V8 engines during World War II and then negotiated Harry Miller's purchase of Fred Offenhauser's racing engine business. Operating with friend and partner Dale Drake, Meyer obtained the engine operation from Offenhauser in late 1946 and continued to manufacture engines of the same design. The company, known as Meyer-Drake, also developed advanced Ford V8 engines for Indianapolis in the 1970s. One of the smartest, most successful engineer-racers in history, Louis "Louie" Meyer finally retired in 1972 and died in Searchlight, Nevada, in 1995, after being inducted into the Motor Sports Hall of Fame three years earlier.

Now unchallenged, with Snyder more than a lap behind, Shaw spotted Meyer's wrecked car and immediately reduced his speed, cruising the final two laps to victory in order to save what little fuel remained in the Maserati tank. His winning speed would be a modest 115 miles per hour, well below the potential of over 120 miles per hour. No matter, it was the second victory for both Shaw and Mike Boyle, who with Henning, had teamed with the late Bill Cummings to win the 500 in 1934. Better yet, Ted Horn brought the second Boyle car home in fourth place, behind Snyder in second and Cliff Bergere in third. This helped counter the impact of Chet Miller's serious injuries, which left him in the nearby Methodist Hospital with several broken bones but in no real danger of losing his life (a fate he would suffer at the track thirteen years later).

After the entire Boyle team had visited their injured teammate, they retired to a catered suite at the elegant Claypool Hotel downtown, where the party rattled the windows until the early morning hours. Mauri Rose, who had artfully driven Shaw's old winning "pay car" to a solid eighth place, was also invited, as was old friend and rival of Louie Meyer. The festivities were tempered by the day's deaths and injuries, which, in that era of colossal bravery and risk taking in the face of constant high-speed danger, remained omnipresent.

As the race fans drifted out the city and headed to all points of the compass in the Midwestern heartland, they remained impervious to the rising tide of war in Europe and the Far East. Both the Nazis and the Imperial Japanese Army were on the march, the latter ravaging China, while Hitler's Wehrmacht was in high-gear training for the so-called Blitzkrieg lightning war that was soon to overwhelm Poland and trigger the most savage conflict in human history. Yet in the midst of the continental turmoil, which was soon to encompass France, a tiny cadre of wealthy sportsmen and one woman based in Paris and in Monaco was planning, of all things, an invasion of the Indianapolis 500. If details could be worked out with the French bureaucracy—who were already halfheartedly preparing for war, based on the silly illusion that the upstart Nazis would be quickly subdued by the Grand Armée guarding the Maginot Line—the Boyle machine's two remaining Maserati 8CTF sister cars would be on the way to Indianapolis to contest for victory in the 1940 Memorial Day extravaganza.

With conflicts ranging from Russia and Finland in the east to Austria in the west, and spreading even to Italy's botched Ethiopian adventures in Africa, the idea that anyone living in Europe in the summer of 1939 could possibly entertain the thought of hauling a pair of race cars to America to engage in an automobile race seemed beyond the bizarre. Yet to a wealthy American expatriate named Lucy O'Reilly Schell, the notion seemed not only feasible but a perfect diversion from the dark days that lay ahead.

9

A FRENCH INVASION

WILBUR SHAW SETTLED into his new job as a spokesman for the Firestone Tire and Rubber Company in Akron, Ohio, while Cotton Henning returned the grease-stained Maserati to his shop for a complete dismantling and repairs in preparation for the 1940 Indianapolis 500. Umbrella Mike Boyle had returned to Chicago and to the business of Electrical Union Local 134, fighting as usual the endless investigations and potential criminal charges from various federal and local law enforcement agencies that knew the rising power of labor unions served as petri dishes for the growth of organized crime.

As Europe teetered on the edge of the abyss that would plunge it into World War II, the aristocracy lived on as if peace were omnipresent. The lavish casinos in Monaco were alive with activity as were the fashionable ski resorts in the French, Italian, and Swiss Alps. Motor racing remained a gentlemen's sport, even among the intensely professional teams fielded by Mercedes-Benz and Auto Union, both of which operated with Nazi financial support, based on propaganda minister Joseph Goebbels's conviction that if powerful German cars dominated the Grand Prix circuit, it would pay dividends not only in public support of Germany's military and political power but also in aiding the technological development of tank and aircraft engines.

Benito Mussolini had also attempted to support the Milan-based Alfa Romeo team, but despite substantial infusions of lire, Italy could not contest the German operations in terms of finances and in performance on the tracks. Riding on the perimeters of government help were the Maserati brothers and the struggling French Delahaye company, which had been building automobiles in its suburban Paris factory since 1894. This operation had, in the late 1930s, challenged the Germans and on one rare occasion had actually beaten the Teutonic powerhouses. But the French government, with typical lassitude and a fascination with the good life, cared little for the international sport and, like the British, let its automobile industry deal with such challenges on its own.

Yet there were wealthy citizens who believed that the sport of motor racing was a valid technical enterprise and the highest form of human competition. Two such people were Laury Schell and his wife, Lucy O'Reilly Schell, members of the so-called Lost Generation, who had moved to France from Reading, Pennsylvania, in the late 1920s, when such exoduses were at the height of fashion. Writer Gertrude Stein was credited with coining the phrase while conversing with fledgling novelist Ernest Hemingway, both to become superstars among the clique of American writers who had emigrated to Paris in the 1920s after the end of World War I. They were joined by such literary giants as John Dos Passos and Sherwood Anderson and the famed F. Scott and Zelda Fitzgerald, who among the literati were socially comparable to the Schells but became vastly more famous in the years to come.

Lucy and Laury's money had come from Lucy O'Reilly's father, an Irish immigrant with a murky background, and was most likely plumbed by mobsters during the Prohibition, when Irish and Italian gangs contested for domination of the contraband liquor market from coast to coast. Loaded with funds from unknown legal or illegal sources, Lucy O'Reilly left America with her new husband, Laury Schell, to take up residence in an elegant Paris apartment and a breathtaking seaside villa in Monte Carlo. The two were fascinated with high-performance automobiles and participated in road rallies and other amateur events in the south of France. They also financed a team of French Delahayes in Grand Prix competition, retaining the brilliant René Dreyfus as one of the team's drivers. He was a native of Nice with a Jewish background, carrying the name of the notorious Dreyfus Affair, which in 1894 had generated a wave of anti-Semitism in France after the accusation that Captain Alfred Dreyfus had allegedly passed French military secrets to the Germans. While ultimately found not guilty, the stigma lingered for years, and although René Dreyfus was unrelated to the denigrated officer, he had to withstand criticism even when in 1938 he had been declared French auto racing champion.

It was Dreyfus, at the wheel of one of the Schells' V12 Delahayes, who had upset the German teams in April 1938. The surprising victory had come on the twisty street circuit at Pau in the south of France, where the more nimble Delahaye had a unique advantage over the powerful but cumbersome German machines. It was this victory plus other successes that made Dreyfus the champion of France—an honor that contradicted the rising anti-Semitism sweeping across the nation and continental Europe as a whole. Lucy O'Reilly Schell and her husband spoke fluent French, but their two teenage sons, Harry and Phillip, spoke no English at all, although the entire family retained dual American/French citizenships. In January 1937 René Dreyfus and Laury Schell had teamed up in their Delahaye Model 135 to finish fifth in the grueling Monte Carlo Rally, establishing a strong union between the great driver and the family.

While racing went on across the Continent under the gathering war clouds of 1938, Lucy became fascinated with the idea of returning to her native land and winning the famed Indianapolis 500 race. Plans were made to bring one of their Delahaye Grand Prix cars to the race in 1939 but were interrupted when Laury suffered an auto accident while driving north from their Monte Carlo villa. Although at first the crash didn't seem to be serious, ultimately it caused paralysis on Laury's left side, forcing risky brain surgery that only partially cured the malady. Even while her husband struggled to recover, Lucy Schell refused to give up her dream of coming to America to compete at Indianapolis. In August 1939, three weeks before Germany invaded Poland and with the entire continent on edge, she drove to Bologna to meet with the Maserati brothers. Her mission was to purchase the two remaining 8CTF Grand Prix cars, chassis 3030 and 3031, sisters to the Boyle machine that Wilbur Shaw had driven to victory at Indianapolis. The notion of purchasing a pair of high-priced, exotic racing automobiles in such a situation seems ridiculous in view of how World War II was soon to begin; nevertheless, Lucy O'Reilly Schell remained totally focused on gaining victory in faraway America, a country that appeared immune to any conflicts that might boil up in the near future.

Germany had already invaded Poland and France, and Great Britain had been at war for nearly two weeks when Lucy Schell arrived at the new Maserati factory in Modena, Italy, on September 14, 1939. By then the Maserati brothers were in dreadful financial shape, having sold most of their interests to the powerful Orsi family of Modena and moving the entire operation from their home in Bologna.

Their two 8CTFs had been campaigned with limited results during the 1939 and 1939 seasons in Europe. A high point had come during the 1939 German Grand Prix at the Nürburgring, when German sports car expert Paul Pietch, at the wheel of chassis 3030—the first of three 8CTFs built in early 1938—shocked the Germans by leading the race until brake problems dropped him to third at the finish. His teammate, Luigi Villoresi, also performed well, in chassis 3031, before spinning off the course without injury or serious damage to the car. A month later René Dreyfus took his first ride in chassis 3030 at the Swiss Grand Prix in Berne, finishing in eighth place. The second car, in the hands of French nobleman Raphael Bethenod, Count of Montbressieus, who raced under the name "Raph," had mechanical troubles and did not start. With the two cars back at the Modena shop, Lucy Schell negotiated with the Maserati brothers and the Orsis to have them repaired, painted the blue international racing colors of France, and shipped directly to America, where they would be entered in the 1940 Indianapolis 500.

Returning from Monte Carlo, she contacted René Dreyfus, who was now in the French army, asking him to drive one of the cars at Indianapolis, with teammate and friend René LeBègue in the other machine. Baffled at the offer, Sergeant Dreyfus argued that it would be out of the question for him to leave his army unit to compete in a motor race in America in the middle of a war! While the French establishment, both military and political, was convinced that the Grand Armée would quickly prevail against the upstart Huns, it was still impossible for Dreyfus to understand how Lucy O'Reilly Schell could possibly pull enough bureaucratic strings to release him from his military duties to make a trip to America in order to compete in an automobile contest—especially with a car constructed in an enemy nation. But Lucy Schell, supremely confident and outspoken to the point of often shocking her petite, adopted French countrymen, assured Dreyfus and LeBègue that, thanks to her connections within the government, come May 1940, not only would France have triumphed against Hitler but the way would be clear for the newly formed "Ecurie Lucy O'Reilly Schell" to easily win America's greatest race.

Almost immediately after returning from Modena with her plans formed for the American invasion, however, Lucy's husband, Laury, was involved in another automobile accident. In early October the Schells were traveling to their Parisian home as passengers in the family's powerful Delage V12 sedan. The driver, their private mechanic, skidded on wet pavement, and the big car hammered a roadside tree head-on, instantly killing Laury Schell and seriously injuring Lucy.

Despite being shattered by the loss of her husband and bedridden for an extended period, Lucy O'Reilly Schell adamantly refused to alter her plans to win at Indianapolis and pledged to field her two Maseratis at the great race on Memorial Day 1940, regardless of her health or the state of the world. Viewing Lucy Schell's near-fanatic urge to race cars at Indianapolis from a vantage point more than sixty years later only makes her plan murkier. Based on the political and economic climates of both France and the United States, her reasoning seems marginally insane. If her plan was purely financial, considering the potential winnings gained in a possible 1–2 finish, it is unlikely that any significant profits might result, based on the costs of purchasing, shipping, and maintaining the two automobiles plus the funding of the drivers and crew. Perhaps her idea stemmed from pure ego—a chance to flaunt her wealth and position in her native land—while the possibility also exists that she planned to run the Maseratis once and then sell them to rich American sportsmen for a huge profit. Whatever her motives, they remain a mystery, even to readers of René Dreyfus's 1983 autobiography, *My Two Lives,* wherein he artfully details the Indianapolis campaign but never reveals (even if he knew) the actual motivation for Lucy O'Reilly Schell's strange urge to compete in the faraway Indianapolis 500 while the world was on the verge of the most savage war in history.

There is little question that her husband's accident and death blurred and altered whatever plans she had initially conceived. Did she intend to return to her native land, based on the conflict spreading across Europe? Or did she expect to win the big race, pocket the money, and return to France? Did she plan to keep the two cars in America for further racing, or to sell them once they had competed in the 1940 500? If she had any firm notions before the purchase of the automobiles, the ensuing tragedy involving her husband must have so altered her plans to a point that any long-term strategies were discarded. But despite the difficulties that entered her life, Lucy O'Reilly Schell refused to cancel her entry of two cars in the Indianapolis 500. Whatever her motives, they are lost to history.

10

ANOTHER VICTORY

THE NEW YEAR of 1940 rolled in with Umbrella Mike on top
of the world. His Boyle Special had won the greatest race
and padded his wallet with more than ten thousand non-
inflated dollars after Shaw and Henning and the crew had
been paid half the total purse (while other teams shared
only 35 to 40 percent). Henning had taken the Maserati to
his Indianapolis shop for a complete tear-down and rebuilding and planned to return to Indianapolis in May with the
team intact. Wilbur Shaw was on the lecture circuit touting
Firestone Tires as he electrified fascinated crowds with his
adventures in racing.

Boyle was back in Chicago, hard at work running his
union and seemingly out of trouble with the law. Better
than ten years had passed since his endless battles with the

feds over his violations of the Sherman Anti-Trust Act that resulted in his short trip behind bars until his pardon by President Woodrow Wilson. There being no doubt about his ragged but constant relationship with the major crime families in the Windy City, and about the unabashed power of his union in the world of construction and maintenance, Boyle still remained free of the law while his prominence—and bank account—expanded as a result of his car's victory at Indianapolis.

Mike's fame actually reached Hollywood when an obscure producer/director name Roy Del Ruth proposed a biographical film based on his life titled, of course, *Umbrella Mike*. But Boyle had always hated the nickname (he actually liked being called the "Flying Harp," based on his Catholic upbringing and his love of speed). He refused to work with Del Ruth, and the project died an early death, so the story of his life never reached the silver screen. He ardently claimed that he had never employed an umbrella to receive bribes and had been given the nickname after leaving an umbrella at a Chicago restaurant and returning to retrieve it. Whatever the real story, after Shaw's victory at Indianapolis, Mike Boyle became a true power broker within Chicago's labor unions and political establishment. When important labor leaders or prominent gangsters became embroiled in legal problems that had them headed for prison, the saying went around the clubs and saloons where such crowds gathered that "Only Mike can save him now."

Then it was Boyle's turn. On February 14, 1940, federal agents knocked on the door of his lavish home on

Chicago's Grand Boulevard, where he lived with his second wife, Helen, in the summer months. During the long Illinois winters, he, Helen, and his two daughters, Eloise and Lois, spent long vacations at their second home on Alton Road in Miami Beach, seemingly far away from the razzle-dazzle world of labor, crime, and power politics. The agents presented him with an indictment handed down by a federal grand jury, again charging Boyle with violations of the Sherman Anti-Trust Act in restraint of the building trades in Chicago. It was similar to the charge that had caused him so much grief from 1921 to 1925.

At age sixty Boyle was living the good life, at least until the indictment arrived. He responded by calling into action his cadre of high-powered lawyers who had defended him and other union members over the years, prompted by occasional wildcat strikes, local blackouts, and endless accusations of links to the highest levels of organized crime. Because the alleged abuse of the Sherman Anti-Trust Act was a serious offense, Boyle slipped away from his racing activities to defend himself. This charge would trigger reprisals by his fellow union members over the next two years. Backed by Democratic politicians in the city and state, Boyle was hardly ready to succumb to the federal action and instead began to pressure local business interests for more, not less, union involvement.

After seeing the fall of Al Capone to the Internal Revenue Service, Boyle understood the sensitivity of his racing activities and the obvious suspicion that it was a shelter of massive dimensions. As the 1940 Memorial Day race came

closer, he judiciously recorded every expense related to the
Maserati and his two key men, Shaw and Henning. If he
was to fight the feds, it would be outside the purview of his
hobby, and despite all the legal wrangling that lay ahead
and the hundreds of thousands of dollars spent in legal
fees, the government agents from the IRS and other
bureaus chasing Umbrella Mike were never able to con-
nect his crime-blemished union efforts to his involvement
in motor sports. When practice for the Indianapolis 500
opened on the first of May 1940, Boyle was not present.
Nor would he be during the entire month, except for the
running of the big race. Legal pressure in Chicago had
become too intense for him to take his traditional May
vacation at the speedway.

It was during that month that nationally syndicated
columnist Westbrook Pegler first placed Mike in his sights,
preparing a typical hard-edged story that would be published in papers across the nation during the months of
July and August. At the time, Pegler was a powerful force
in American media, operating both in print and on the
radio with right-wing polemics that spared no one. His col-
umn led off in typically pugnacious fashion: "Here is
another certified crook whom you may file away in your
rogue's gallery of extortionists, thieves, and traitors who
enjoy the protection of the Wagner Act [a pro-union law
passed during the Roosevelt New Deal] and a Supreme
Court decision in their racketeering and traitorism in this
hour of national peril." Like many in the media, Pegler was
sounding the alarm relating the rising wars in Europe

and the Far East and was convinced that the isolationism and lackluster military preparation by the politicians in Washington bode for disaster.

After recounting Boyle's troubles with the U.S. Circuit Court of Appeals in the 1920s and again repeating their denouncement of Boyle as a "blackmailer, a highwayman, a betrayer of labor and a leech on commerce," Pegler completed his assault by connecting Boyle to his counterpart in the IBEW union in New York, Harry Van Arsdale, accusing both of blockading important war work. Pegler accused Boyle of preventing the installation of lighting fixtures in a Flint, Michigan, Buick plant that was building U.S. Army Air Force bombers. Pegler's assault marked the first time Mike Boyle became a national figure. But thanks to powerful political support and ironclad power within his union, Boyle barely flinched, even as the feds moved closer.

Linked by telephone to Henning and Shaw, he monitored what was going on at Indianapolis Motor Speedway as the Maserati took to the track, now considered by the racing establishment to be the car to beat in the upcoming 500. From the moment the race cars rolled onto the speedway, three men dominated competition. Rex Mays, the lead-footed crowd favorite from Riverside, California, had taken the wheel of retired Louie Meyer's big Winfield-8 Bowes Seal Fast Special and appeared to have the pole position locked up. But Shaw, in the Boyle Maserati, was hard on his heels, as was Mauri Rose in a new, Offy-powered machine, built by Los Angeles craftsman Curly

Wetteroth, that was essentially a sister to the car Floyd Roberts had driven to victory in 1938.

It did not take long for the grim reaper to make an appearance. Veteran George Bailey, who had labored long and hard to make Harry Miller's radical, four-wheel-drive, rear-engine Gulf-sponsored machines competitive, hit the wall during a practice lap on May 4. With the car carrying its fuel in unprotected tanks on the sides of the chassis, the Miller exploded instantly, burning the helpless Bailey to a crisp. Decades would pass before race drivers would be protected from fire, with both special Nomex driving suits and foam-packed containers for the fuel. Understanding that such incidents were simply part of the price of admission, the rest of the drivers carried on with a kind of gallows humor that shielded their fear or remorse for poor Bailey. As expected, when qualifications were ended, Mays held the pole, with Shaw second and Rose third in the Lou Moore–entered Offy.

The two sisters of Shaw's 8CTF did not fare as well. Lucy O'Reilly Schell's planned invasion of Indianapolis had hit a horrible snag with the death of her husband, Laury, in October 1939. Still recovering from the injuries she suffered in the accident, Lucy remained at home in Monaco while her little team—composed of her two drivers, René Dreyfus and René LeBègue; her chief mechanic, Luigi Chinetti; and her nineteen-year-old son, Harry— made the trip to America. They somehow slipped away from war-torn Europe for what seemed to be a frolic of speed in faraway, isolationist Indiana.

The French team was greeted with great hospitality. Track owner Eddie Rickenbacker and Wilbur Shaw were among the contingent who met them at the Indianapolis airport, while the two Maseratis rolled in on May 24 aboard a B&O railroad car. Shaw was particularly helpful to Dreyfus and LeBègue, neither of whom had ever driven on an oval like Indianapolis and, worse yet, were used to racing in a clockwise direction, unlike the American fashion of making left-hand, or counterclockwise turns. Neither Frenchman spoke English, and but after a few early runs Dreyfus nevertheless voiced his hatred for the speedway, which, unlike the twisty, European road courses, involved four high-speed sweeping turns and a pair of long, 170-mile-an-hour straights. Moreover, the steering on the two O'Reilly Schell Maseratis vibrated badly, like the Boyle car, and Henning helped chief mechanic Chinetti install the same hardwood stiffeners that he had employed with success on his own machine.

Early in practice the LeBègue car, with Dreyfus at the wheel, suffered terminal damage when its crankshaft broke. There being no replacement, the engine was taken from the Dreyfus car. The car made the thirty-three-car starting field in qualifications (qualifying runs being another surprise for the Frenchmen, who were accustomed to automatically placing in the starting field with a drawing position). LeBègue was to drive the first 250 miles and then turn the car over to Dreyfus for the final 250. Although Shaw qualified the sister 8CTF 3032 at over 127 miles per hour, LeBègue was almost five miles an hour slower against the stopwatches and barely made the field in thirty-first spot.

A third Maserati qualified in twenty-fourth place, driven by Argentinean sportsman Raul Riganti, who had somehow obtained one of the more advanced and radically improved 420-horsepower 8CL Maseratis from the factory. But a lack of preparation of the car and Riganti's inexperience doomed the machine to a backmarker status, ending when Riganti crashed on the twenty-fourth lap of the race. His car slammed the retaining wall, rolled over twice, and flung the driver onto the soft infield grass, which, as with Louie Meyer a year earlier, permitted him to survive with only minor scratches and bruises. Riganti returned to Argentina, never to appear at Indianapolis again.

Like many foreign race drivers who came to Indianapolis, Riganti had no doubt underestimated the challenge imposed by the giant 2.5-mile rectangle. Being used to racing on open road circuits that traversed city streets and open country highways, Riganti, LeBègue, and Dreyfus came to Indianpolis believing that circulating a track employing only four constant-radius left-hand corners ought to be simple. Little did they understand that each corner was a quarter mile in length, demanding that the driver operate on the ragged edge of control for one mile each lap, during which the slightest bobble would cause a spin and contact with the stout retaining walls lining the circuit. Moreover, the cornering speeds of 110 to 115 miles per hour were significantly faster than many of the straightaway speeds required on many European road courses. Add the fatigue experienced over the five-hundred-mile distance and the constant jockeying with the other thirty-two competitors, and the entire challenge at Indianapolis was greater and more daunting than any first-time visitor might expect.

Journalists in the European motoring press were inclined to deride Indianapolis as a "big left turn," implying that running in a single counterclockwise direction was somehow simple. But with the stout cement retaining walls of the speedway little more than an elbow length away and the high-speed velocities necessary to remain competitive over such a long distance, dozens of European race drivers came to Indianapolis and found themselves daunted by the immense rectangle. Suddenly the notion of simply "turning left," when it involved four giant corners for two hundred laps and two straightaways where speeds of 160 to 170 miles per hour were needed, became a truly scary enterprise. Some Europeans, like early winner Jules Goux (1913), Ren Thomas (1914), and Dario Resta (1924), had done very well during the early years of the race. But as speeds increased on the high-banked board speedways of the 1920s, American drivers gained confidence running at constant high speeds and developed a dominance at Indianapolis. Most of the top European drivers remained on the Continent, not returning until the 1960s.

Mike Boyle had again managed to get his three-car team into the starting field, with future star Ted Horn starting fourth and newcomer Frank Wearne in seventh, both behind the wheels of the Boyle team's aging machines, which had little hope of performing with the leaders.

On race day, May 30, 1940, Rex Mays arrived with low nimbus clouds scudding over the track and rain forecast for the entire Midwest. But the Hoosier multitudes pouring into the Brickyard had only the weather to worry about, while across Europe citizens of Denmark, Norway, Holland, Belgium, and France were facing the dark specter of Nazi domination. The northern half of Europe was in German hands, and on May 29, one day before the race began, 200,000 members of the British Expeditionary Force and 140,000 defeated French soldiers had gathered on the beaches of Dunkirk for evacuation to England, huddling from incessant German air raids and long-range artillery bombardment. Within less than a month France fell, to be seized by the Vichy government, which was sympathetic to the Nazis, therefore removing the Grand Republic from the conflict. This left only battle-scarred Great Britain and Russia to face the German Blitzkrieg.

When the green flag dropped at Indianapolis on Memorial Day 1940, Rex Mays surged into the lead, with Rose and Shaw trailing in his wake. Shaw's disciplined style was to never let the Maserati at its limit in the early stages, so he let Mays set the pace while he held back in order to make a hard charge for victory during the final one hundred miles. Mays's driving on the edge caused extra tire wear and a long pit stop, during which Shaw took the lead, driving smoothly while keeping both Mays and Rose at bay. Meanwhile, LeBègue was using the power and handling of the Schell Maserati with considerable skill. At the halfway mark he had passed more than a dozen competitors, and when he gave up his seat to the jittery Dreyfus, the team was in a position to possibly make a late charge for the lead—a seemingly impossible task considering their starting position at the rear of the field.

But all such plans were canceled by the weather. At the 375-mile mark the clouds released their moisture in the form of a fine drizzle. Unlike European road racing, where competition continued despite the weather, the American Automobile Association, which governed the Indianapolis 500, forbade racing in the rain. This prompted track officials to wave the yellow flag, slowing the pace and forcing the cars to remain in place, with no passing permitted. That would lock the standings until the rain stopped and the track dried. At that point Shaw was in first place, Mays in second, Rose third, Horn fourth, and Wearne, in the other Boyle car, was sitting in seventh. Dreyfus had managed to move the Schell Maserati into tenth place, where he puttered through the shower in frustration, as did Mays, both of whom were planning a hard charge at the finish to overtake Shaw.

The screwball life of Joel Wolfe Thorne had taken another downturn, forcing the two Sparks-built Little Sixes to be parked in the midst of another financial firestorm and a raging dispute between Thorne and car builder–designer Art Sparks. This had left Thorne able only to enter his aging Big Six for himself, while the two faster machines were forced to remain in Sparks's Los

Angeles shop. This marked Thorne's fourth appearance in the 500, having finished a creditable seventh the year before. He had qualified at tenth for the present race, and when the rain began to fall he was in fifth place—his best finish in nine appearances at Indianapolis before dying in a private airplane crash in 1955.

Lap after lap unwound in the increasing rain with no chance of resuming the competition. The two hundredth lap—or five hundred miles—was completed with Wilbur Shaw and the Boyle Maserati cruising to an effortless victory, Shaw's third and the car's second straight. It was an unusually uneventful day for the Boyle team once the rain had begun, although during a late-race pit stop Shaw had run over Henning's right foot as he accelerated away, breaking a small bone. The famed mechanic arrived at the Victory Lane celebration with a noticeable limp and his face tense with pain.

After a wild celebration at Boyle's hotel suite and a sharing of the prize money, the boss climbed into his big Packard convertible and headed back to Chicago. Exhausted from his weekend away from the union wars, but always eager to drive at high speeds on the highway, Boyle made cautious preparations in case he fell asleep at the wheel. When taking long motor trips, especially between his Chicago and Miami Beach homes, he softened the right side tires. Should his car veer onto the shoulder while dozing, Boyle figured, the clatter of rumpled rubber on the rough gravel lining the highway would instantly wake him. But being as energized as he was after his cars once again dominated the greatest automobile race in the world, this trip caused him no trouble. He arrived back in Chicago to face yet another battle in the upcoming wars that endlessly swirled around IBEW Local 134 and its now-famous leader.

Meanwhile, the Dreyfus/LeBègue team was preparing to break up, having won fourteen hundred dollars for their tenth-place finish and feeling reasonably satisfied with their performance. But the future looked bleak, considering the collapse of France and being, in essence, hung up in a foreign land without a country while seeing newspaper photos of the hated swastika flying over their beloved Eiffel Tower. After exchanging repeated cables with Lucy Schell at her home in Monaco, it was decided that the two Maseratis had to be sold, since there were no races scheduled in Europe for the foreseeable future. California car builder and former race driver Lou Moore made a low offer of fifteen thousand dollars for the pair (about one-quarter of their combined value), and it was reluctantly accepted. With one car carrying a badly damaged engine, there was little choice but to take Moore's deal. Lucy O'Reilly Schell's American campaign had resulted in a disastrous financial loss.

Dreyfus, LeBègue, Chinetti, and young Harry Schell left for New York, where they moved into the luxurious Savoy Plaza Hotel and spent several days visiting the New York World's Fair on Long Island. Rene Dreyfus's wife and brother Maurice remained in Paris, as there was no possibility of joining—them, especially for a Jew who, in theory, was still in the French army. René Dreyfus arranged to purchase a small restaurant in rural New Jersey and then hooked up with a wealthy New York socialite by the name of Emelyn Pearlman. Dreyfus would later join the American army and, after the war, would team up with Maurice to open the famed Le Chanteclair restaurant on Forty-ninth Street in Manhattan. During the 1950s and 1960s it became a watering hole for motor sports and auto industry celebrities from around the world.

Luigi Chinetti also settled in New York, taking a job as a master mechanic at the prominent J. S. Inskip imported car dealership in Queens. After the war he became the East Coast distributor for the new high-performance sports and racing cars being built in Modena, Italy, by former driver Enzo Ferrari.

Now widowed and with her only son, Harry, in faraway America, Lucy gave up her Paris apartment and took refuge at her Monaco villa. Despondent and alone, she lived out the war in the neutral principality, safe from the violence that spread across Europe but forever separated from the glamorous world of motor sports that had energized both her and her late husband for so many years. Drinking heavily and increasingly mired in elegant isolation, she dreamed of once again returning to her native land, but she died at age fifty-six before the war ended. Despite her death and that of her husband, the two Maseratis that had brought them brief fame would remain a part of their heritage, even to this day.

Harry Schell eventually learned enough English to join the American army for the duration of the war. He then returned to his homeland and began a racing career of his own, financed by his mother's fortune. A talented driver, Schell competed in major sports car events in Europe and in Grand Prix competition, gaining a reputation as a playboy and a vivid character on the international motor sports scene. In a strange bit of irony, the wildly superstitious Schell died on Friday, May 13, 1960, at Silverstone, England, when he lost control of his Cooper Grand Prix car in heavy rain and hit a stone barrier, being killed instantly.

The O'Reilly Schell invasion at Indianapolis could hardly be described as a triumph, but considering the impact that both Dreyfus and Chinetti had on American motor sports and the ongoing involvement of the two Schell Maseratis at Indianapolis, which would last for well over a decade, Madame O'Reilly Schell produced surprising, if unexpected, long-term results.

11

WILBUR'S LAST RIDE

WILBUR SHAW WAS now being celebrated from coast to coast as the only man to win consecutive 500s, but he harbored unspoken personal frustrations over his newfound prominence and bulging bank account. Both Indianapolis 500 victories, in 1939 and 1940, had come under the yellow flag, with his competitors unable to make a final challenge in the closing laps. Whether he and the Boyle Maserati would have been able to once more withstand the assaults of men like Rex Mays, Jimmy Snyder, Mauri Rose, and Ted Horn, remained a moot question never to be answered.

As the preparations for the 1941 race were being made by Henning and his Boyle crew, Shaw understood that this would probably be his final race, one way or the other. War clouds hung over the entire world, and each day the press blared news of Germany and Japan's increasing aggressiveness. It seemed inevitable to most Americans that even with the great ocean forming a vast, liquid Maginot Line, that barrier was bound to be breached and the nation would become involved. Now in his late thirties, it seemed certain that Shaw would be too old to compete again if the race were canceled for an uncertain duration that might last for years. This reality only increased his intense urge to cap his long and successful career with an unprecedented third consecutive victory at Indianapolis—this time running the entire five hundred miles at top speed to the checkered flag.

Wilbur Shaw was a national celebrity, and in the summer of 1940 he had been featured in a full-page magazine advertisement for Camel cigarettes, a leading brand for the R. J. Reynolds Tobacco Company. Smoking was considered highly fashionable, and several decades were to pass before the link between tobacco and lung cancer was firmly established. Camel, Lucky Strike, Chesterfield, Pall Mall, and other well-known brands were major advertisers in magazines like *Life, Look,* and the *Saturday Evening Post* and on network radio (ten years before television replaced it in terms of media impact). A color ad showed Shaw in the seat of the Boyle Maserati holding a Camel cigarette surrounded by actors serving as journalists. Although he did not smoke heavily in real life, the ad quoted Shaw as testifying, "Camels burn slower and give me the extra mildness and extra flavor I want for steady smoking. Camels give me extra smoking." Within twenty years the government would clamp down on such lunatic hyperbole about the dangerous weed, and cigarette advertising would essentially disappear in major media. For some time, however, it would remain a presence in automobile racing, with the Winston brand sponsoring major stock car racing in the southern United States.

Umbrella Mike was back in the headlines in February 1941 when he once again called for his bridge workers to raise thirty-two of the bridges over the Calumet River into their upright positions. Fifty traffic lights in the heart of the city's Loop were also turned off during the morning rush hour. The dispute lasted for five hours while union and city negotiators battled over the financial issues. The strike was eventually settled, but by then Umbrella Mike had made the deep impression on the citizens of America's second largest city that he possessed the power to bring the economy to halt any time he felt his union was threatened.

Even as he was still embroiled in union warfare, Boyle found the time, energy, and resources to fund Henning's preparation for the 1941 Indy 500. The Maserati had been disassembled completely down to the last nut and bolt. After every part had been examined and judged fit for the pounding, Cotton Henning and his small crew had carefully rebuilt the big red machine, totally confident that it was capable of not only running the distance, but leading the field to the finish. Others clearly believed they could defeat the Boyle team, including Rex Mays in the powerful Bowes Winfield-8, plus Mauri Rose, who would drive one of the former Schell Maseratis now owned and entered by Lou Moore. Young Chicago ace Duke Nalon was assigned to the other Moore-Schell Maserati but would have trouble in qualifying and would never be a contender. Two of Shaw's former rivals were not present—Louie Meyer having retired, and Jimmy Snyder dead after a racing crash at a minor track in Illinois. Joe Thorne, still in financial trouble, entered only his Big Six for himself, while his two other Sparks-engineered cars remained locked up in California.

Amazingly, René LeBègue was back, having somehow returned to France in the middle of the war and obtained a Talbot-Lago Grand Prix car. Using bribes and smuggling techniques that remain a mystery, he managed to sneak the car across the French border into Spain, where it was shipped by freighter to New York and on to Indianapolis. The machine, totally unprepared for the big speedway, was unable to qualify, averaging only 116 miles per hour, or 14 miles an hour slower than the pole-winning speed of Mauri Rose, who had quickly adapted to the Moore-Schell Maserati now sponsored by the Illinois-based Elgin Piston Pin Company.

For the first time since they had been built four years earlier in faraway Italy, the three 8CTF Maseratis were together, ready to contest in the Indianapolis 500. The Boyle car remained the favorite, with Shaw starting in third position beside Rose and Rex Mays. This meant two of the three great machines were sitting in the front row when the green flag dropped. Aside from Mays in the big Winfield, there seemed to be no American car with any

chance of beating the two Maseratis of Shaw and Rose—
that is, until several strange twists of fate scrambled the
race like no other in history.

Race day morning had exploded in warm sunlight
across the entire state of Indiana. As usual, the crews had
been working in Gasoline Alley before dawn making final
preparations on the automobiles for the upcoming 500,
scheduled as usual to begin at 11:00 a.m. (Central Standard Time), with an expected finish somewhere around
four in the afternoon. This presumed an average speed of
about 115 miles an hour, to be slowed by probable long
periods of caution to clean up the omnipresent wrecks. At
just past seven o'clock, the crew of George Barringer's
Miller—the sister car to the one that had taken the life of
George Bailey the year before—was filling its side tanks
with the regular pump gasoline that the new rules required
for all competitors. Several garages away, a mechanic—
never identified—lit a blowtorch to make a quick repair on
one of the other race cars. The gasoline fumes from Barringer's machine had crept along the floor, serving as a
fuse to engulf the Miller in flames. Within seconds the fire
had leaped to the rafters of the old wooden building.
Crews madly pushed their cars into the open air and frantically scrambled to save their tires and tools that clut-
tered the work areas. The local fire department responded
quickly, but not before the building was a charred ruins.
Amazingly, only Barringer's car among the thirty-three
entrants was destroyed, while two other unqualified racers
being stored in the garage were also burned to the ground.

As firemen from the city of Speedway and other Indianapolis units soaked down the ruins, the crews poked through the wreckage in search of lost items, both personal and mechanical. The race would be delayed for almost two hours while the teams regrouped and inventoried what they had salvaged. Henning had managed to get the Maserati clear of the fire, along with the spare wheels and tires to be employed during the race. But the torrents of water that had been poured onto the flames had washed away his chalk marks on the Firestone tires that identified them as "RF" for right front, "LR" for left rear, and so on after they had been specially balanced and fitted for such placements. One Borrani wire wheel had been found to be defective with loose spokes and had been marked "Do not use." But such notations had been erased by the fire hoses, and unbeknownst to Henning, the rejected wheel had been placed among those to be used during the race.

Even though the car and its gear had been saved, Wilbur Shaw was personally upset by the fire. In the melee his favorite pair of driving shoes had been lost. Like most drivers of the day, such good luck charms were as critical to him as safe tires and a proper running engine in the grand schemes of things. Depressed and feeling somehow naked in the face of the contest he faced, Shaw donned a fresh pair of brogues and prayed for the best.

The field lined up, three by three, with the usual competitors ready to fight for the win. Mauri Rose, who had quickly adapted to driving the former Schell Maserati, was on the pole, with Shaw on the outside, separated by Rex Mays in the Winfield-8 that had been vacated by Louie Meyer the year before. Only thirty-one cars would take the green flag, as Barringer's Miller was fried to a crisp, and young Sam Hanks, an expert California midget driver, had crashed late in practice after qualifying and was recovering in Methodist Hospital.

Ted Horn had abandoned Umbrella Mike's team and taken the seat in one of Joe Thorne's Art Sparks–built Little Sixes. Thorne had managed to wrangle enough money from his estate to enter Horn's car, which the young Ohio driver had qualified in fourth place. His eccentric boss had returned with his favorite Big Six and managed to make the field in twenty-third place. Horn had already told friends that despite his car's vaunted power, he hated the handling.

Boyle had two other cars in the field, with now-recovered Chet Miller starting ninth and newcomer George Connor, who had replaced Horn, in the thirteenth slot. Sitting in seventh on the grid was veteran Hollywood stuntman and race driver Cliff Bergere, who planned to run the race nonstop in his Wetteroth dirt track car that had been fitted with an extra-large fuel tank. Only one man had gone the distance nonstop before—Dave Evans in a Cummins Diesel-powered machine in 1931, finishing thirteenth while averaging an impressive sixteen miles to the gallon. Bergere, in top physical condition, had calculated that a steady run minus the long periods consumed in the pits would bring him victory from his seventh-place starting position.

Also in the field, in nineteenth place and under a dark cloud, was 1935 500 winner Kelly Petillo at the wheel of an aged dirt track machine known as the Airlines Sandwich Shop Special. He would last just forty-eight laps before the car broke down, and he then disappeared from the sport. A tough little criminal with numerous arrests, Petillo would later go to prison on a charge of attempted murder unrelated to his racing career. While most American drivers had come from working-class backgrounds, amazingly few, like Petillo, crossed the line into the world of crime. Some had engaged in driving bootleg liquor during the Prohibition, while others in the early days had been accused of fixing races, but a vast majority vented their aggressions on the racetrack and not against fellow citizens, save for the occasional barroom brawls or post-race fistfights. But overall, considering the combative nature of their profession and the overt macho quality it demanded, the number of competitors who were arrested for serious crimes was exceedingly small. A difficult character, Petillo never returned to the sport after his release from jail, and he died of natural causes in 1970.

While Lou Moore and his crew had concentrated their efforts on Mauri Rose's Maserati, he had a backup in the field sitting in the seventeenth starting position. Veteran Midwestern dirt track driver Floyd Davis had run four times in the big race with little success and was not considered to be a serious contender for a high-place finish, much less a victory.

The stench of burnt rubber and fried metal having wafted out of Gasoline Alley from the horrific fire only hours earlier, the thirty-one remaining cars were now lined up under the sunny skies for the twenty-ninth running of the fabled event. Aside from Duke Nalon, who was deep in the field in the second Moore Maserati, the contenders were all bunched up front, with Shaw an outright favorite to become the first man to win the 500 three times in a row, while both Rose and Mays beside him seemed certain to win the big race before their expected long careers would end.

Five laps after the green flag was waved, the field remained a swarm of multicolored mechanical wasps buzzing for position. Mays took the lead, and Rose dropped back to third behind Shaw, surely testing the handling of the unfamiliar Maserati in the heat of battle. Then Lou Tomei, a midfield starter, spun out as he entered the sweeping third turn at the end of the long back straightaway. Directly behind him was Joe Thorne in the Big Six, who had no choice but to slide into Chicago driver Emil Andres. Both cars slammed the outer retaining wall, crumpling metal and tossing wheels into the air, but somehow the two drivers were left intact. Both cars were out of the race, but Andres and Thorne walked away from the wreck uninjured. Their accident brought out the caution flag for thirty laps while emergency crews cleaned up the mess. During this period Rose gained confidence with his Maserati, and when the race resumed, he sped past Shaw and Mays to take the lead. But his charge would quickly be ended when the Maserati's ignition system failed—no doubt a result of sluggish running under the yellow flag— and Rose retired, an angry and frustrated man who felt victory was in his grasp. He grabbed car owner Lou Moore and demanded that he be allowed to take over teammate Floyd Davis's car, now dawdling along in fourteenth place. Meanwhile, Shaw, driving with typical smoothness, had taken the lead from Mays and seemed headed for another unprecedented victory. The race had settled down until the seventy-second lap, when Davis was called in by Lou Moore and told to give up his seat to Rose. A brief argument ensued before Davis sullenly climbed out and Rose leaped in and thundered out of the pits.

Shaw and Mays had made their first pit stops and were back at speed. But suddenly the scenario changed forever. Sailing into the first turn away from the giant grandstands lining the front straight, Shaw felt the Maserati twitch to the right. The big car started a slide toward the wall, its rear wheel collapsing under the strain. Unable to correct quickly enough against the failed wheel, Shaw slammed the retaining wall backward at over 140 miles an hour, knocking him unconscious and tearing up the rear suspension and tail of the car. With the caution flag flying, emergency crews lifted Shaw from the cockpit as he screamed in agony. He was carefully lifted into an ambulance and hauled off to Methodist Hospital while the giant crowd sat in stunned silence. The greatest driver in recent history was suddenly in peril, with his vaunted Maserati now stuffed against the concrete retaining wall, its sleek tail rumpled like a wad of newspaper.

As the wrecked car was hauled off the track and into the garage area, Shaw was already being x-rayed in the hospital's emergency room. Three of his vertabrae had been cracked in the impact. With his wife and friends now in attendance, Shaw was fitted with a cast and given a private room. He was to remain in the plaster prison for more than two months before he was declared healed. But the team of doctors warned Shaw that further injuries to the fractures could result in the complete paralysis of his legs. It was during this long recovery as he approached his thirty-ninth birthday on October 13 that Shaw realized his long and illustrious career behind the wheel of a racing car—especially Umbrella Mike Boyle's marvelous Maserati—was finally over.

Back at the Motor Speedway, Shaw's Maserati had been cleared away, Cliff Bergere had taken the lead, and Rex Mays and Mauri Rose were riding hard on his tail. Driving like a madman in a car not considered to be ideally suited for racing at Indianapolis—having been designed primarily for running one-mile dirt tracks—Rose began to surge toward the front. Running nonstop according to his plan, Cliff Bergere had gained the lead with fewer than fifty laps remaining. But engine fumes and the pounding on the rough track had exhausted him and Rose surged past. Ironically, both Bergere and Rose were driving nearly identical cars built by Curly Wetteroth. Meanwhile, Rex Mays struggled to keep up in the ill-handling Winfield, and Horn, riding in fourth, battled the cranky Thorne Sparks machine in similar fashion. Fatigued to the brink of unconsciousness, Cliff Bergere hung on as his pace slowed, dropping him to fifth place at the end of the race, while Mauri Rose sped onward to his first victory in the 500.

When the race was over, Floyd Davis loudly told the press that he had been about to make his own charge for the lead and would have won without Rose's efforts. His claim was generally ignored, in that he was bogged down in fourteenth place when Rose took over with no apparent ability—or urge—to improve his position.

Even if Mike Boyle's day had ended with his star driver in a body cast and his best car battered, he had the limited satisfaction of knowing that his veteran backup driver, Chet Miller, had finished sixth, while George Connor had retired with transmission failure at 167 laps and ended up sixteenth in the standings.

Despite the disappointment of losing his star driver and having his best car shattered, Mike Boyle made plans for the 1942 Indianapolis 500—a race that because of World War II never happened. The Maserati was taken to Henning's shop and was easily repaired, with only the aluminum tail and rear suspension needing treatment by the master mechanic and his talented crew. Shaw eventually recovered, but it was clear that another driver would replace him for next year's race. Obviously a number of talented drivers were awaiting the call, based on the potency of the Boyle Maserati and the strong organization beckoning its annual campaign at the great Indianapolis Motor Speedway. But all such planning was based on the presumption that the big race would be run as usual the following May, a presumption that dimmed with each passing month as the world plunged toward total war.

Only forty-two cars had appeared at the speedway for qualifications as the nation steadily moved toward a full war effort. Involvement in Europe seemed inevitable, with ally Great Britain desperately hanging on and Russia under a major assault by the Germans. But little did anyone expect that America would be pulled into the great conflict—not by the Nazis, but by the Japanese navy and air force. At the moment the 1941 Indianapolis 500 ended, major air and sea maneuvers were under way off the Japanese main islands in preparation for a sneak attack on Pearl Harbor scheduled for December 7. This would mark what President Franklin D. Roosevelt called a "day of infamy" that would alter the world forever and drop sporting events like the Indianapolis 500 into the footnotes of history.

From 1942 through 1945 Indianapolis ceased to be a center of motor racing as the great city became immersed in the war effort, building Allison aircraft engines by the thousands for both the American and British air forces. The giant company had been founded by James A. Allison, one of the founders of Indianapolis Motor Speedway in 1909 and one of Indiana's leading citizens. The Curtiss-Wright Corporation, builders of the P-40 Warhawk fighter plane—made famous by the Flying Tigers—also had a factory in the city. But the company's main plant was in Buffalo, New York, an industrial center near the birthplace of aviation pioneer and company founder Glenn Curtiss in Hammondsport, New York, where he had engaged in his early test flights on nearby Keuka Lake.

During the war the giant speedway was used for limited tire testing and military vehicle evaluations, but was essentially left to decay, with weeds thriving between its bricks and its massive grandstands beginning to sag through misuse. But the track was too much of a cultural and economic icon for the city and the entire state of Indiana to die. As America and its allies began to crush first Germany and then Japan, it became obvious that Indianapolis Motor Speedway would gain new life as soon as victory was declared.

12

THE RAVAGED POSTWAR YEARS

THE MOST SAVAGE conflict in the history of mankind dragged on, with tens of millions dead, until the second atomic bomb was dropped on the Japanese industrial city of Nagasaki on August 9, 1945. During those years, when gasoline was rationed and America was on a total war footing, the last thing on the minds of Hoosiers was their beloved Indianapolis 500. Eddie Rickenbacker had long since lost interest in the aged track and was running Eastern Airlines. Wilbur Shaw, at forty-two and too old for military service, remained with Firestone as aviation sales manager during the war effort and sometimes tested U.S. Army tires at the speedway.

When peace arrived, Shaw convinced Terre Haute, Indiana, millionaire Anton "Tony" Hulman, whose family produced Clabber Girl Baking Powder, to purchase the speedway from Rickenbacker for $750,000 and to hire Shaw as the president and general manager in hopes of reviving the big race on Memorial Day 1946. Hulman's purchase ended plans advocated by some city officials to convert the speedway property into an industrial park.

Mike Boyle had stored the Maserati in Chicago for the duration, and when the race was announced for Memorial Day, he rehired Cotton Henning to once again prepare the machine for the event and offered Ted Horn the chance to replace the retired Shaw. Horn, who had learned his trade on the tough dirt tracks in California, was considered a major talent. He and Henning were already friends, and the young, handsome man who had come from a wealthy family in Cincinnati knew that the big machine had enormous potential to win the Indy 500, despite its age. In fact, it was among some of the more modern cars to return to Indianapolis when practice opened on the first of May 1946.

The ravages of the Great Depression, coupled with the war effort, had stymied construction of anything as frivolous and expensive as a racing car. Many of the automobiles that appeared at the speedway that spring were dated to the early and mid-1930s, with a number tracing their heritage to the 1920s. Only Lou Moore among the first rank of owner/builders seemed to be countering the static situation. Having gained investment money and sponsorship from the Blue Crown Spark Plug Company, he did not appear at the track, choosing instead to remain in Los

Angeles to construct a pair of front-drive, low-slung, Offen-hauser-powered machines that would be ready for the fol-lowing year in the hands of Mauri Rose and teammate Bill Holland. They were destined to dominate the 500 in 1947, 1948, and 1949.

Lou Moore's Blue Crowns were hardly the only threats to the domination of the Boyle Maserati. In 1941 Detroit manufacturer Lou Welch, a close friend and business asso-ciate of Henry Ford's, had commissioned the Winfield brothers, Ed and Bud, with the aid of the brilliant Cali-fornia draftsman Leo Goosen, to design and create super-charged V8s that for the next twenty years would dominate Indianapolis in terms of raw horsepower. The 550-horse-power engines—installed in two complete cars that fol-lowed in 1946—were known as the Novis, named for the small Michigan city that was Welch's residence. Fitted in front-drive chassis created by Frank Kurtis, and first driven by fifty-two-year-old veteran Ralph Hepburn, the prototype Novi was radically faster than all other entrants in the 1946 500 but failed to finish. The power and erratic han-dling of the Novis would take the lives of both Hepburn and Chet Miller, as well as badly burning another top-flight driver, Duke Nalon, over the career span of the famed machines (with multiple variations in design), which lasted until they were finally retired in 1960.

During the late 1940s and early 1950s, cars like the Lou Moore Blue Crowns and the Welch Novi were considered to be the ultimate in Indianapolis race car design. Their front-wheel-drive layout seemed ideally suited to the four smooth, sweeping speedway corners, which eliminated the need for a driveshaft, which in turn reduced their weight and bulk. But the cars were tricky to drive, possessing latent understeer (the front wheels losing traction before the rears) that gave the drivers little latitude when negotiating the turns. Both Ralph Hepburn and Chet Miller—established veterans in their fifties—lost their Novis in nearly identical crashes. Entering the third turn at the end of the back straightaway, they nosed onto the grass verge on the inside of the track and then applied power to get back on course. In both cases, the brutishly powerful car snapped to the right and drove headlong into the outer retaining wall, killing their driver instantly.

In 1952 Frank Kurtis introduced the "roadster" design, a rear-drive machine with the driveshaft beside the driver, permitting a lower center of gravity and better weight distribution. This type of automobile was to dominate the 500 until European rear-engine machines replaced them a decade later. These new designs—front-drive Blue Crowns, Novis, the Kurtis roadster, and English Coopers and Lotuses—left the Boyle Maserati in the dust. Yet its potential for winning survived longer than any single automobile at Indianapolis.

As practice opened for the first postwar 500, in May 1946, the Maserati was eight years old. It had dominated three of the last races before the beginning of World War II, winning twice. Despite its age and the fact that its superstar driver, Wilbur Shaw, was retired, the classic old veteran was still considered a major contender.

Ted Horn was pleased with the Maserati, now painted a lurid lavender with white trim and number 29 on its hood, replacing the number 2 carried by Shaw in his final drive. Horn had first run the 500 in 1935 and from 1936 through 1941 had established an amazing record of consistency, finishing second once, third twice, and fourth four times. Highly intelligent, he was considered a certainty to win the big race before his career ended. Running cautiously with an unfamiliar car, Horn qualified the Boyle Maserati in seventh place, while stuntman Cliff Bergere, at the wheel of the Wetteroth dirt track car he had run nonstop in 1941, won the pole position.

The Bergere machine, like many in the race, had a strange history that was pockmarked with triumph and tragedy. This was the same car that Floyd Roberts had driven to victory in 1938 and then died in it a year later. After being repaired by owner Lou Moore, it was sold in 1941 to Bergere, who drove it nonstop to finish fifth. In the 1946 race Bergere was to lead early, but retired after eighty-two laps with engine trouble.

The winner of the 1946 Indy 500 was young British émigré George Robson, a talented California transplant, who drove one of Joe Thorne's Sparks Little Sixes. This would mark the first and only time that one of Thorne's automobiles won the big race. He had already sold the sister car, and, short of cash again, had in desperation offered the ride to Robson, a driver with only two dismal performances in the race (twenty-third in 1940 and twenty-fifth in 1941). As a winner at Indianapolis, Robson's career blossomed, and Bergere offered him the seat in his Wetteroth car for the remainder of the 1946 AAA season, which would be contested on one-mile dirt tracks around the nation.

On September 2 Bergere and Robson took the car to a one-hundred-mile race to be run on the dusty mile track at Lakewood Speedway outside Atlanta, Georgia. Early in the race Robson was involved in a multicar pileup that killed both him and fellow driver George Barringer (at the wheel of Wilbur Shaw's ancient "pay car" that had carried him to his first Indianapolis victory in 1937). This was shattering news for Shaw, in that he had employed the "pay car" nickname to the machine because it had produced so much revenue, thanks to its Indy victory and its seventh-place finish the year before after leading the race before the hood blew off. He had built the car in a California shop and had qualified it among the fastest cars at the 1936 Vanderbilt Cup, only to stuff it into a fence on the second lap of the race.

Hauling Robson's bent and bloody machine back to his shop in Indiana, a distraught Bergere seized a welding torch and later told friends, "Floyd Roberts and George Robson—both winners at Indianapolis, died in this car. That's two too many." Bergere then lit the torch and cut the car to pieces.

Though Robson had won the 1946 500, Ted Horn finished third with the Boyle Maserati, his pace slowed by haunting magneto troubles. But feeling confident that he could win the big race with the machine, he signed on for 1947.

Mike Boyle felt differently. With three victories in the 500 notched in his belt and the constant pressures of the union—and the government—with him day and night, he decided to end his involvement in big-time automobile racing. After long meetings with his friend and partner Cotton Henning, Boyle made arrangements to sell the Maserati. A pair of Texas oilmen, Gene and Leo Bennett, became the sponsors, although historians believe the car was sold directly to Cotton Henning. Ted Horn agreed to remain with the car for the 1947 race.

Again Horn was doomed to finish third. After qualifying the Maserati on the pole position, he led the race in the opening laps. But after several long pit stops, the two new Blue Crown Spark Plug Specials, owned and built by Lou Moore and driven by Mauri Rose and Bill Holland, went on to finish first and second.

A year later the result was nearly a duplication, except that Horn, in the Maserati—still sponsored by the Bennett brothers, but now officially owned by Cotton Henning— dropped to fourth place at the end, while the Blue Crowns once again ran first and second.

Based on his winning the AAA National Championship, during the 1946 and 1947 seasons Horn had raced the aging Maserati with number 1 on its hood, the same number the machine had carried in 1940. No other automobile in the history of the Indianapolis 500 ever carried that honored number even twice, much less three times, while being driven by such talents as Wilbur Shaw and Ted Horn. Those superb drivers, backed by the brilliant hands of

Cotton Henning and the Maserati brothers in faraway Bologna, established Mike Boyle's prize as the single most successful car ever to run at Indianapolis and perhaps anywhere in the history of motor sports.

Then it was over. On October 10, 1948, Ted Horn, the popular national driving champion, took his favorite dirt track car, which he called "Baby," to the one-mile dirt track at DuQuoin, Illinois. In those days, no Magnaflux or other metal fatigue analysis was required. Running hard for the lead, as he entered the second lap Horn's front axle fractured, sending the machine into a violent tumble and tossing Horn out. He died twenty minutes later on the way to a nearby hospital.

Unlike many of his working-class compatriots, Horn was educated to become a professional musician like his father. He attended exclusive private schools and studied music, art, and poetry—hardly qualifications for becoming a professional racing driver. Even in his later years he read poetry and on occasion played the piano for friends. He was raised in Hollywood, California, where the family expected the handsome young man to enter the bur-geoning motion picture industry. But by age fifteen he was racing jalopies on Los Angeles dirt tracks and soon was driving professionally. At eighteen he tried to make the grade at the insanely dangerous Ascot Speedway near Los Angeles and had a serious crash. At that point his father banned him from the sport, and he spent the next four years learning the trade of photo engraving. He then returned to Ascot and immediately crashed again. But he adamantly refused to stop racing and by the mid-1930s was considered to be a major future talent.

The circumstances surrounding Horn's death remain a puzzle. Although he was known to be wildly superstitious about the color green, not shaving the day of the race, refusing to be photographed the day of the race, carrying a lucky dime in his right boot, and adopting other peculiar habits, it was later discovered that on the morning of the DuQuoin race, he had shaved and let his wife, Theresa (his fourth, who was pregnant with his only child, a daughter), wear a green dress to the track. He also posed for pictures with a small group of children, and even stranger, when the coroner removed his clothes, it was discovered that his lucky coin was in his *left* boot. Moreover, he had told his friend Wallace J. Comfort, nicknamed "Jughead," who served as a sort of good luck presence for Horn, to stay home in New Jersey that day. This all left many to wonder if Horn had a premonition and accepted the inevitable.

Among the many people in the racing fraternity who were devastated by Ted Horn's death was his close friend Rex Mays. After attending Horn's funeral, Mays carried on with his racing career, but many of his associates noted that he was less enthusiastic and sometimes seemed to lapse into a deep funk before a race. Like Horn and others, Mays adamantly still refused to wear a seat belt, recalling an earlier crash at the high-banked dirt track in Dayton, Ohio, when his car had plummeted over a sixty-foot embankment. Having been thrown from the car before the plunge, Mays used the incident as an argument for never staying with a crashing car. But during a November 11, 1949, race on the finely manicured one-mile horse track at Del Mar, California, Mays lost control of his Wolfe Special and was launched onto the loamy surface. Having flown P-38 fighter planes in World War II, Mays liked to drive in a khaki-colored flight suit. But, as recorded in a horrific two-page sequential photo spread in *Life* magazine, it was apparent that Mays's prostrate figure blended into the dirt surface, making him invisible to oncoming cars. Veteran Hal Cole later tearfully claimed he never saw the unconscious Mays and ran over him, killing the famed driver instantly.

Ironically, the fatal race had been organized and sponsored by Mays's good friend, the famed singer and actor Bing Crosby. A known horse racing enthusiast, Crosby also loved cars and the sport of automobile racing. But after witnessing the death of Rex Mays, he abandoned motor racing and the Del Mar event was never run again. Crosby's guilt was enhanced in that his race had been added to the AAA schedule late in the season and Mays had not planned to compete. But because of Crosby's persuasion, Mays made arrangements to bring Erwin Wolfe's Kurtis-Kraft to the event only as a courtesy to the Hollywood idol.

Four years later Chet Miller, who had also run regularly for Mike Boyle, was killed while practicing for the Indianapolis 500, affirming the gruesome statistic that until new safety measures such as seat belts, fireproof clothing, roll bars, and better helmets, were adapted in the 1970s, fully *one-third* of all the drivers who competed in the Indianapolis 500 were doomed to die in racing accidents, making it arguably one of the most dangerous sports or professions in the world.

Not only did the deadly automobiles of the day take lives, but many in the sport had a penchant for private flying, and this, too, produced tragic results. One day before his fifty-second birthday, Wilbur Shaw, still the best known and most respected man in American automobile racing, was returning from a business meeting in Detroit to his home in Indianapolis. Shaw had visited the Chrysler Corporation's new proving grounds in Chelsea, Michigan, where he had test-driven one of the prototype, high-powered Chrysler 300 coupes. He had flown in earlier that day with his close friend Ernest Roose of Indianapolis, a painter of portraits of the Indy 500 winners for L. Strauss & Company. Ray Grimes of Greenfield, Indiana, was the pilot of the rented single-engine Cessna as they left the Detroit Metro Airport on the afternoon of October 30, 1954.

The sky was overcast, with a ceiling of less than one thousand feet as the Cessna climbed to a cruising altitude of six thousand feet, where the ambient temperature was two to three degrees below freezing, based on reports from other pilots in the area, who were reporting icing conditions on their wings. About fifteen miles south and east of Fort Wayne, Indiana, Grimes called the local Baer Airfield asking if there were any holes in the cloud formation that would permit him to make a visual landing. The report was negative, prompting Grimes to request an instrument landing, which was granted immediately. That was the final word from the airplane until frantic calls arrived at the Decatur, Indiana, police station that a light plane had crashed shortly after four o'clock in a cornfield on the edge of the small city. Emergency crews arrived to find a totally destroyed aircraft containing the bodies of Shaw, Roose, and Grimes. While no definitive reason for the crash was determined, it is believed that the icing finally coated the wing and tail control surfaces, causing Grimes to lose control. The Midwest was plunged into mourning, as one of its true heroes was dead. After a massive funeral, a service area on Interstate 80/90, the Indiana Turnpike, was named for Shaw, as were numerous memorials around the state of Indiana.

Among the many great figures in America motor sports, Wilbur Shaw remains a giant. His victories on the racetrack and his Olympian efforts to revive the famed Indianapolis 500 after World War II have raised him to iconic status, while his famed Boyle Maserati remains the centerpiece of the beautiful, much-visited Hall of Fame Museum on the grounds of the Indianapolis Motor Speedway.

The year 1955 will be remembered as the worst year in automobile racing history, with the terrible crash at LeMans that killed nearly one hundred spectators, and with the death of champion Bill Vukovich, who, like Wilbur Shaw, was on his way to a third consecutive victory at Indianapolis. The year also brought the death of Shaw's old rival, Joe Thorne. On October 17 Thorne took off alone from the Burbank, California, airport in his Beechcraft Bonanza. Moments later he nose-dived into an apartment house in North Hollywood, killing the eccentric racer and three occupants of the building, and critically injuring several others.

Cotton Henning retired from racing and sold the Maserati after the 1948 Indy 500—no doubt a reaction to the death of his friend Ted Horn. But the car remained active in the hands of a group of Indiana sportsmen who formed Indianapolis Race Cars, Inc. Future 500 champion "Mad Russian" Bill Vukovich had taken his first ride at the speedway at the wheel of the ancient machine. He failed to qualify, as did several other struggling newcomers who tried the car in 1951 and 1952 before chassis 3032 was retired and restored in its famed Boyle motif and placed in the speedway's museum. Its last serious outing came in 1949 when upstate New Yorker Lee Wallard took the wheel of the aged machine, at the time owned by a consortium of Indianapolis businessmen. Wallard made the starting field in twenty-third place but lasted only fifty-five laps before the transmission failed. Two years later Wallard would win the 500 in another brand-new American-built machine, while the old Maserati slipped into the shadows before its restoration and recovery.

The two other 8CTF Maseratis of Lucy O'Reilly Schell also remained around the speedway scene, but after Ted Horn's fourth-place finish with the old Boyle car in 1948, none of the trio was able to compete seriously. In 1951

West Coast driver Bud Sennett crashed chassis 3030 in practice, and the final 8CTF appearance came in 1953 when its Pennsylvania owner/driver Joe Barzda brought chassis 3031 to the speedway but was too slow to qualify.

At that point the three Maseratis left big-time competition. Today the two former O'Reilly Schell cars have been restored and are in the hands of prominent vintage car collectors Joel Finn, who owns chassis 3031, and Miles Collier, who has chassis 3030 in his superb private Florida museum. They are occasionally exhibited at car shows and concours d'elegance around the nation. If any of the trio were ever to be sold, experts in the vintage car collector world estimate that the two O'Reilly Schell machines would each be worth upward of three million dollars, while the Boyle car is valued at least five times that much, making it one of the rarest and most desired automobiles in the world.

Somehow the three Thorne Engineering cars avoided the junkyard fate that ended the career of most obsolete racing cars. The Little Six that George Robson drove to victory at Indianapolis in 1946 is in the Indianapolis Motor Speedway Hall of Fame Museum, and its sister is in racing historian Joseph Freeman's collection in Boston. The Big Six is in the collection of enthusiast David Uihlein in Milwaukee, while the car that Mauri Rose won with in 1941 is also in the Indianapolis Motor Speedway museum, as is the Louie Meyer Bowes Seal Fast Winfield-8 (minus the engine). The fabled Shaw "pay car" is believed to be in Illinois, perhaps unrestored and, in cowboy parlance, after a long cattle drive, "rode hard and put away wet."

Although most of the Indianapolis cars of the 1930s and 1940s were generally raced into the ground before being cut up (many for World War II scrap drives), others, like the three Maseratis and the Thorne cars, were saved and are now prized components of American motor sports history. It is believed by collectors that others exist, packed away in barns and sheds, waiting to be discovered and restored. The value of such machines, once their provenance is confirmed through research and full and accurate restorations are completed, is sure to escalate in the future. The search goes on.

Ironically, in the same year that Ted Horn died, fifty-three-year-old Harry "Cotton" Henning passed away in Independence, Missouri, from a heart condition. Upon Henning's death, his eighty-two-year-old mother received a letter from another former Independence resident: President Harry Truman wrote, "I am shocked and saddened by the news of the untimely passing of your devoted son. He was my faithful friend for more than 30 years. To you and all of those who mourn with you, I offer this assurance of heartfelt sympathy in which Mrs. Truman joins." The pallbearers at Henning's funeral included Wilbur Shaw, and messages of condolences and flowers were received from many friends, including Mike Boyle.

The Maserati brothers are long since gone, although their name remains a vital component of the vast Fiat automobile empire. After being taken over by Argentinean entrepreneur Alessandro DeTomaso, the Maserati company blundered through several postwar decades until it was absorbed into the Agnelli family's giant Fiat automobile operation. Today Maserati manufactures a tiny quantity of high-priced exotic road cars but has no direct involvement with the type of motor racing that elevated the marquee to immortality at Indianapolis and in Grand Prix competition. The day when the word "Maserati" struck fear into those planning to compete in the Indianapolis 500 has long since been forgotten, only to be recalled by those who study the history of motor sports or visit the Indianapolis Motor Speedway Hall of Fame Museum.

Despite the fact that Umbrella Mike remained away from the auto racing wars, his union troubles continued to mount. In June 1949 Edward J. Brown, the former president of the International Brotherhood of Electrical Workers, sued Boyle and the IBEW for one hundred thousand dollars, claiming he had been barred from the organization. At the time, Boyle was serving as vice president of the union's sixth district in Chicago, but the charge nevertheless singled him out as the man who had kept Brown out of the organization. The suit was settled out of court for an undisclosed amount of money.

Three years later Boyle made the headlines again by urging the nation's union workers to reduce their workweek to thirty hours. He cited the fact that peacetime production had been cut from the hectic war years, although the Korean War was now at its height. He proposed that the then-current five eight-hour workdays be reduced to five five-hour shifts with no reduction in pay. Boyle's demand made headlines in some Midwestern newspapers but was ignored in Washington.

Ironically, Umbrella Mike outlived them all. His end came on May 17, 1958, at the Miami Heart Institute. While spending the winter with his wife, Helen, at their Miami Beach home, he had been stricken with a heart attack four days earlier. His wife, two daughters, and seven grandchildren, were with him when he passed away. The wire stories that carried news of his death around the nation mentioned his nickname, but they also noted the fact that he had long since discarded his famed umbrella for a cane. At the time of his death, at age seventy-seven, he remained vice president of the IBEW and business manager of IBEW Local 134. Its headquarters at 600 West Washington Boulevard in Chicago were closed on May 22, 1958, in memory of its longtime leader, and Boyle's funeral at St. Mary of the Lake Roman Catholic Church was attended by hundreds of its loyal members. He was buried in the family plot in Chicago's Mount Olivet Cemetery beside his first wife, Minnie. He was survived by his second wife, Helen, two daughters, seven grandchildren, two sisters, and a brother.

Shortly thereafter, men like Mike Boyle, who engaged in motor sport purely as a hobby, became rare. Factory-backed entries of cars in the Indianapolis 500 cost millions of dollars, with little chance of reward. Men like Wilbur Shaw, who drove unprotected with pure instinct, had been replaced by men in space suits who were more engineers than drivers, dependent as they were on exotic aerodynamics and sophisticated suspension systems that could not be overcome with raw talent. So, too, for instinctive mechanics like Cotton Henning, who tended to deal with machines like Boyle Maserati's as living creatures, massaging them as a trainer would a racehorse. Today technicians treat such machines as temporary, disposable devices with no personality, pedigree, or provenance.

The days of Umbrella Mike, Wee Wilbur Shaw, and Cotton Henning are long gone but never to be forgotten. Each in his own way contributed to the incredible growth of motor sports in America, which now rivals the National Football League in popularity. Wilbur Shaw remains a legendary figure at the Indianapolis Motor Speedway, having dominated the place behind the wheel of his Maserati before becoming its postwar chief executive while elevating the five-hundred-mile race to the largest single-day sporting event in the world. Umbrella Mike, a difficult and controversial individual at best, somehow managed to shrug off his dark side in Chicago crime and union skullduggery to bring into play his splendid maroon Maserati, which remains the single most successful racing car in the Indianapolis speedway's history. To be sure, Umbrella Mike Boyle was in many ways an unsavory character, but his commitment to automobile racing—and to the Indianapolis 500 in particular—helped to propel the sport beyond the Great Depression into the highest levels of popular American culture.

Somehow this team of Boyle, Shaw, and Henning, operating in strange concert with the Maserati brothers in faraway Italy, offered a respite to the daily drudgery of many Americans who were rising from a decade of economic disaster and unknowingly facing another five years of savagery fighting the most brutal and bloody war in the history of mankind.

This is hardly to imply any nobility in their efforts to simply win an automobile race, any more than other idols of the day like Yankee star Joe DiMaggio, the great horse Seabiscuit, the incredibly popular book and movie *Gone with the Wind,* crooner Bing Crosby, and other cultural icons altered the course of history. But in their intense world of big-time automobile racing, Umbrella Mike Boyle, the classic union tough guy from Chicago; all-American Hoosier hero Wilbur Shaw; and the mechanic genius Cotton Henning combined their diverse talents with a group of Italians to lead their beloved sport into new heights of popularity.

Today, a half century later, automobile racing rivals professional baseball and the National Football League in popularity and commercial impact. The growth of NASCAR (National Association of Stock Car Racing) in the United States has been unprecedented in the world of sports, with such events as the Daytona 500 and the Charlotte World 600 attracting millions of enthusiasts either through actual attendance or via live television broadcasts. But although its dominance in terms of popularity has eroded somewhat due to NASCAR's overwhelming growth, the Indianapolis 500 remains a Memorial Day icon.

One can only imagine the level of prominence that

would be enjoyed by Wilbur Shaw and Umbrella Mike Boyle if they were dominant today rather than in the Depression-ravaged 1930s and late 1940s. But to the thousands of visitors who swarm the Indianapolis Motor Speedway Hall of Fame Museum each year to ogle the totally restored Boyle Maserati—carrying its maroon design of 1940—the wild days of Umbrella Mike, Wilbur Shaw, Cotton Henning, and the Maserati brothers in faraway Italy remain vibrantly alive.